Student Workbook

for use with

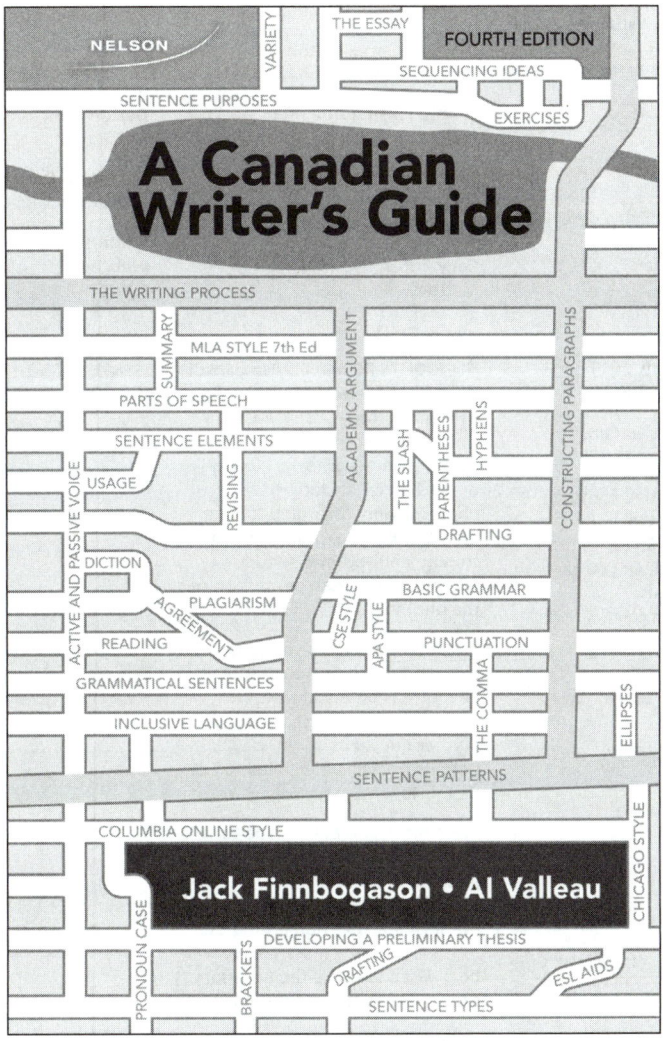

Prepared by JACK FINNBOGASON

and AL VALLEAU

NELSON EDUCATION

Student Workbook for use with
A Canadian Writer's Guide,
Fourth Edition

by Jack Finnbogason and Al Valleau

Vice President and Editorial Director:
Evelyn Veitch

Editor-in-Chief:
Anne Williams

Executive Editor:
Laura Macleod

Marketing Manager:
Amanda Henry

Developmental Editor:
Theresa Fitzgerald

Permissions Coordinator:
Joanne Tang

Senior Content Production Manager:
Natalia Denesiuk Harris

Copy Editor:
Matthew Kudelka

Production Coordinator:
Ferial Suleman

Design Director:
Ken Phipps

Managing Designer:
Franca Amore

Printer:
Webcom

COPYRIGHT © 2010, 2005 by Nelson Education Ltd.

Printed and bound in Canada
1 2 3 4 12 11 10 09

For more information contact Nelson Education Ltd., 1120-Birchmount Road, Toronto, Ontario, M1K 5G4. Or you can visit our Internet site at http://www.nelson.com

ALL RIGHTS RESERVED. No part of this work covered by the copyright herein may be reproduced, transcribed, or used in any form or by any means—graphic, electronic, or mechanical, including photocopying, recording, taping, Web distribution, or information storage and retrieval systems—without the written permission of the publisher.

For permission to use material from this text or product, submit all requests online at www.cengage.com/permissions. Further questions about permissions can be emailed to permissionrequest@cengage.com

Every effort has been made to trace ownership of all copyrighted material and to secure permission from copyright holders. In the event of any question arising as to the use of any material, we will be pleased to make the necessary corrections in future printings.

ISBN-13: 978-0-17-647486-7
ISBN-10: 0-17-647486-2

Contents

Part I THE WRITING PROCESS 1
Chapter 2 Prewriting II: Techniques 1
Chapter 3 Prewriting III: Skill Development 13

Part II ACADEMIC WRITING 33
Chapter 9 The Summary 33

Part III RESEARCH ESSAYS 35
Chapter 15 Step 3: Conducting Research 35

Part IV DOCUMENTATION 39
Chapter 21 Avoiding Plagiarism 39
Chapters 22–25 MLA, APA, Chicago, and Columbia Online Styles 47

Part V BASIC GRAMMAR 51
Chapter 27 Parts of Speech 51
Chapter 28 Phrases and Clauses 55

Part VI SENTENCE ELEMENTS 64
Chapter 29 Parts of Sentences 64
Chapter 30 Sentence Patterns 69
Chapter 31 Identifying Sentence Types 71
Chapter 33 Sentence Variety 73

Part VIII GRAMMATICAL SENTENCES 77
Chapter 41 Construction 77
Chapter 42 Agreement 87
Chapter 43 Common Sentence Problems 100

Part IX USAGE AND DICTION 110
Chapter 44 Diction (Word Choice) 110
Chapter 45 Pronoun Case 118
Chapter 46 Pronoun Choice 121
Chapter 48 Inclusive Language 124
Chapter 50 Active and Passive Voice 126

Part X PUNCTUATION 129
Chapter 52 The Comma 129
Chapters 53 and 54 The Semicolon and the Colon 132
Chapter 55 Quotation Marks 135

Chapter 56 The Apostrophe 138
Chapters 57, 58, and 60 The Slash, Parentheses, and the Dash 140
Part X Punctuation Review 143

Part XI MECHANICS 146
Chapter 63 Capitalization 146
Chapter 64 Abbreviations 150
Chapter 65 Numbers 152
Chapter 66 Hyphens 155

Answer Key 157

Part I THE WRITING PROCESS

Chapter 2 Prewriting II: Techniques

The following is the background for an extended series of exercises. The intention of the exercises is to give you practice in applying the various prewriting techniques discussed in Chapter 2. Because it is impossible to apply these techniques in a vacuum, the next part supplies background on the selected subject for the exercises, **American Idol,** *the television series that has had an extended run near the top of the pack among evening shows. The eventual goal of applying prewriting techniques to this subject is to write an essay on some key facet of the cultural phenomenon known as the* **Idol** *series. If you want to get additional background on that series, "Google" it. You will find, as we did, an extensive Wikipedia backgrounder that will assist you. Below you will find a general summary of the* **American Idol** *series, its history, and its characteristics.*

Backgrounder: *American Idol*

The series known as *American Idol* has now entered its eighth season and continues to be an entertainment and cultural phenomenon. Beginning its life as a summer replacement in 2002, *American Idol* barely made it to a first showing. As Wikipedia relates, the head of Fox Television, Rupert Murdoch, listened to his daughter, Elizabeth, who had loved the British version of the show, and approved its purchase, rejecting the advice of his company's experts. From that humble beginning, the *Idol* series—one of a number of programs dubbed "reality shows"—has grown to be the top draw on American television, moving from a #30 ranking in the summer of 2002 to #1 in 2006. More significantly, it is a cultural phenomenon, having spawned a Disney copy of the show, performed live at

Disney World, a playground in Orlando, Florida; spinoff *Idol* shows in many other countries; and an audience for its broadcasts of some 100 countries, with live showings in places like Canada, Australia, and Israel and delayed showings in countries as diverse as Malaysia and the United Kingdom.

Equally intriguing is that tens of thousands of entertainers audition at regional competitions in the beginning stages of the *Idol* show, despite knowing that only a few will make it through each regional audition. The rules limit the contestants to American citizens, or people holding green cards, between the ages of 16 and 24 (raised to 28 in 2005). Contestants also have to prove their "amateur" status by proving that they hold no contracts or formal agreements with management or record companies, though not every contestant has been forthcoming about this requirement. One of the strongest draws of the *Idol* shows is the simple but suspenseful provision of four rounds of competition— a preliminary, a semifinal, a final, and a finale—to arrive at a single winner. Also, in the American tradition of "rags to riches," the prize is large—a million-dollar recording contract with 19 Management. In five to eight months an unknown singer can become the Idol of the Year, record a single, and have that single soar to first place on the Billboard charts, with all the sales such a ranking guarantees. Clearly, the mythic dimension—and one of the hooks that draw audiences up to 40 million viewers in the United States—is this simple variant on the American Dream: the movement from poverty to wealth, from anonymity to fame, in a short space of time.

A closer look reveals that the year's *Idol* champion is not the only winner in this television monster. In 2007, a year when *American Idol* enjoyed #1 ranking on television, a thirty-second commercial on the show cost $700,000. When we consider that a television "hour" is really only fifty to fifty-two minutes, and that a number of the year's shows are two hours in length, you get some sense of what the show is worth to Fox. The acerbic British judge from the show, Simon Cowell, is reported to have said that 19 Entertainment has already made in excess of $100 million from the recordings of the winners and of the runners-up in this series. If you add together what Fox and 19 Entertainment collectively earn annually from this one show, you may come to believe that this is the central dimension of the *Idol* phenomenon.

That brings us to a dimension of the series that is not as widely known: 19 Management owns 19 Entertainment, and 19 Entertainment owns FremantleMedia, the producer of the show for Fox. Not surprisingly, FremantleMedia also owns the distribution rights for the show. Clearly, the major winners in the *Idol* series are Fox and 19 Entertainment. In fact, 19 Entertainment launched the show as a means of uncovering new singing talent for its link to a major recording company, Sony/BMG. Every applicant who is auditioned must sign a contract with 19 Entertainment running from the date of the audition (usually in September) to three months following the end of the show—a span of up to twelve months. Clearly, this process could tie 7,000 to 10,000 aspiring entertainers to contracts with a single company for an entire year.

This brief sketch of the *Idol* phenomenon suggests several things: a process that for some is entertainment is for others a life-changing opportunity; what for major sponsors is an "ideal audience" profile is for a contestant "precious votes"; and, finally, what for many is a dream or myth made incarnate is, for a few, a business proposition.

Exercise 2-1 Applying the Pentad

Use the Pentad technique as a prewriting tool to prepare for writing an analytic essay on the American Idol *series. In doing so, you will have to think about what the "agent," the "action," and the "agency" are here. "Scene" may initially appear straightforward, but there are complexities to that term as well. Obviously, the "purpose" of this action might become your central concern if you were to go ahead and write the essay. Below you will find space provided for each of the Pentad's terms. Please write your notes in the space provided. Feel free to include questions as well as decisions. Think of this as generating material for the analytic essay you have been asked to write.*

Step One

ACT

_____
_____
_____
_____
_____
_____
_____
_____

AGENT

_____
_____
_____
_____

AGENCY

SCENE

PURPOSE

Step Two

Now apply some selected "ratios" to the task of developing your analysis of the ***American Idol*** *series. Doing this will extend the depth of your work on the individual Pentad terms. Try linking some terms to the "purpose" of the "act" and see what you discover. Then explore the other relationships captured in the additional ratios cited here.*

ACT-PURPOSE

AGENT-PURPOSE

AGENCY-PURPOSE

Exercise 2-2 Mind-Mapping

In your application of the Pentad to the subject **American Idol,** *you will have made some preliminary decisions about the purpose of the show. Whether you think purpose is the limited one of making money for Fox and for 19 Management or the complex interaction of various features that have created* **American Idol's** *great success, you will have made preliminary decisions about the analysis you are about to write. This provides a suitable occasion for mind-mapping the subject. In the space provided below, sketch your map of this subject.*

As additional material for your mapping, consider the following. The televised **Idol** *series begins with auditioning and preliminary trials, proceeds through a semifinal and a final, and concludes with the finale. The decision on the show about winners and losers is made by a panel of four judges (three before the 2009 season), all of whom have become well-known: Paula Abdul, Randy Jackson, Simon Cowell, and the newly appointed Kara Dio Guardia. The final determination is made by public vote. The program is produced by Fremantle Media, a subsidiary of 19 Entertainment, and broadcast on Fox Television. The number of votes submitted by the public is typically greater than the number of viewers. Three of the* **Idol** *winners have made more than a million dollars through their recordings.*

Remember that your map will begin with a central circle surrounding your subject. Feel free to use a larger piece of paper if the one provided will not contain your map.

OPTION

You may wish to try a different approach. You can do multiple maps by placing a different factor in the **Idol** *series at the centre of each mapping. You could, for instance, place the Producer/Broadcaster in one centre, the Entertainers in another centre, and the Audience in a third centre. Because they form the centres of their maps, your mapping will likely produce different results. You can supply your own paper for these mappings.*

Exercise 2-3 Applying Topic Analysis

Topic Analysis is a prewriting technique that can refine your understanding of a topic through the application to your subject of a standardized set of questions. Let's assume that you have already discovered that, while it is easy to define the "act" involved in your subject, the Idol *series, it is not as easy to define the agent and the agency. What is the "agent" behind the show? What is the "agency"? If the agent is the producing and televising companies, the purpose is to make money. However, Fox and 19 Management make their profits in different ways, so you would need to dig deeper into the "agency" behind the show. If the agent is the auditioning singers, then your analysis will move in a different direction.*

At this stage, you may want to deepen your understanding of your subject by applying the topics and conducting analysis. The following exercise helps you do that. For each of the following selected topics, write out your answer. You may also wish to choose which topics you want to apply here instead of applying the ones we have chosen.

CIRCUMSTANCES SURROUNDING THE EVENT OR PROCESS

_____
_____
_____
_____
_____
_____
_____
_____

Chapter 2 *Prewriting II: Techniques* 11

WHO OR WHAT WAS AFFECTED BY THIS EVENT/PROCESS?

IS THE EVENT/PROCESS GOOD? BAD? BY WHOSE STANDARDS?

TO WHAT OTHER EVENTS IS IT CONNECTED?

Chapter 3 Prewriting III: Skill Development

Exercise 3-1 Applying Causal Analysis

Causal Analysis is one of the most useful thinking skills. We have been applying this skill from an early age, slowly developing our ability to assess the reasons behind an event or phenomenon. One approach to refining that ability is to think of causes as belonging to one of two groups. The first group of causes can be sorted in terms of time. Specifically, what are the causes of an event that are close to it in time? Further away? For convenience, we can divide causes with a time relationship into those that are immediate, intermediate, or remote from the event we are examining. Simply listing causes under these headers will generate a first development in your analysis. A second tool organizes causes according to their relative importance in producing the effect or phenomenon. Three kinds of causes in this group are contributory, necessary, *and* sufficient. *As the terms suggest, "necessary" and "sufficient" imply greater importance than we would attach to "contributory." Normally, we cannot define the sufficient cause of an event without including multiple causes. A narrower grouping isolates causes that are necessary from those that are not. The simplest way to begin a causal analysis is to list causes under time categories and then evaluate the relative roles these causes play in the causal chain.*

In this exercise you are asked to analyze the causes behind the success of the American Idol *series. From its inception, this program has been consistently at or near the top in terms of ratings. Why? The following divisions of the exercise ask you to first sort the causes behind this success into different groups.*

IMMEDIATE CAUSES

The term "immediate" in this context creates some problems. After all, the program was well into its eighth year by 2009. It should be enough to respond here in terms of the first two years of the *Idol* series, well before it had created imitation shows in other countries and become a part of our language. Focus here on the causes that first attracted a significant audience.

INTERMEDIATE CAUSES

These would include causes dispersed through the years of the *Idol* series.

_____

_____

_____

_____

_____

_____

_____

_____

_____

_____

_____

_____

_____

_____

_____

_____

_____

_____

REMOTE CAUSES

These would include causes that could even have existed before the first *American Idol* show was broadcast. Assessing remote causes is one of the most important elements in causal analysis, in part because such causes are often important even though not close in time to the actual phenomenon being analyzed.

NECESSARY CAUSES

A necessary cause is one that has to be present if the event or phenomenon is to occur. In other words, such causes are central, and choosing them will test your understanding of the event you are analyzing. Obviously, the presence of a large and loyal television audience is a necessary cause, but you may not believe it is a sufficient cause.

SUFFICIENT CAUSE

Here is your key test. What causes are sufficient to automatically create the huge success achieved by this television program? You may want to review the discussion of causal analysis in Chapter 3 before answering here.

Exercise 3-2 Working with Inferences

In the following exercise you will be asked to complete the final stage of an inference. Two factual statements are supplied to you. You are asked to make a reasoned inference as a product of those two statements in the space provided. In a few instances, you may be asked to provide more than one inference.

1. a) In the early 1970s, approximately 30% of families had one income earner.

    b) By 2005, 70% of families had two income earners.

    _____
    _____
    _____

2. a) Starting around 2004, the American government began offering cash subsidies to farmers willing to devote land to growing crops—corn in particular—that could be used to create biofuels.

    b) Within two years, the price of corn had risen dramatically, making it almost impossible to use as cattle feed or as an export commodity.

    _____
    _____
    _____
    _____
    _____

3. a) The Conservative government of Canada stated, on different occasions, its opposition to running a deficit budget.

    b) In 2009 the Conservative government tabled a budget that called for a deficit rising to $54 billion in three years.

    _____
    _____

4. a) A number of prominent newspapers in the United States have had to close in the past two years.

b) In Canada, the average daily circulation fell by 5% between 2007 and 2008.

5. a) Today's newspaper readers read their chosen paper in both a print and an online version.

b) The combined Canadian readership (online and print) for 2008 is identical to what it was in 2003.

6. a) In B.C. as well as in other provinces, the requirement for public-sector workers to retire at age 65 has been dropped.

b) Approximately 10% of workers in B.C. over the age of 65 continue to work at present.

c) Approximately 70% of university professors at Simon Fraser University in B.C. have continued working after the age of 65 following the cancellation of mandatory retirement.

INFERENCE ONE

INFERENCE TWO

7. a) Most public-sector workers are on a salary schedule that delays full pay until the worker has moved through five to seven annual salary steps.

   b) Therefore, the older workers in a public-sector enterprise generally enjoy the highest salaries and often comprise the largest labour expenditure for an employer.

8. a) Lee Valley Tools, an Ottawa-based firm, caters to gardeners and people engaged in woodworking and home-improvement projects. Lee Valley Tools began life as a mail-order firm.

   b) In 2009, Lee Valley Tools opened a store in Victoria, B.C., its fourteenth Canadian store and its first store on Vancouver Island.

Chapter 3 *Prewriting III: Skill Development*

9. a) In the late 1990s and early 2000s, students often had to have a GPA in excess of 85% to get accepted at a postsecondary institution.

b) In recent years, most postsecondary institutions haven't even checked the Grade 12 or 13 marks of applicants. Some universities grant acceptance to Grade 11 students on the basis of their academic standing, more than a year ahead of when the student can actually attend the university.

INFERENCE ONE

_____
_____
_____
_____
_____

INFERENCE TWO

_____
_____
_____
_____
_____

10. a) Until about three years ago, bottled water constituted the highest product sales at postsecondary institutions, outselling pop, juices, and energy drinks.

b) More recently, bottled water has lost favour with many students and postsecondary employees. In 2008, for the first time, the gross sales of bottled water in Canada declined.

_____
_____
_____

Exercise 3-3 Writing the Inference Paragraph

This exercise asks you to work with an inference in a larger format. At the beginning of the exercise, you will be given some facts drawn from a recent study reported on by Maclean's. You will then be asked to create two inferences from these facts and write them up in two separate paragraphs employing different structures.

Backgrounder

The following data were reported in the April 7, 2009, edition of *Maclean's* in a table on page 43, which is reproduced here. The data were compiled by Project Teen Canada under the leadership of its director, Reginald W. Bibby of the University of Lethbridge.

	1984	1992	2000	2008
Roman Catholic	50%	41%	39%	32%
Protestant	35%	28%	22%	13%
Other faiths	3%	10%	14%	16%
No faith at all	12%	21%	25%	32%

Note: "Other faiths" includes Aboriginal, Buddhist, Jewish, Hindu, Sikh, and Muslim.
Source: Reginald W. Bibby, *The Emerging Millennials* (Lethbridge: Project Canada Books, 2009), 176.

Paragraph #1

Please structure your first paragraph so that your inference is stated first. The rest of this paragraph will state the facts on which your reference rests. You may also have to include the reasoning you employed to draw the inference from these facts.

Please write the paragraph in the space provided.

Paragraph #2

Please structure your second paragraph so that the facts are given first and the inference you have drawn from these facts is given last. Again, you may have to include the reasoning that allows you to draw your inference form this particular set of facts.

Please write this paragraph in the space provided.

Exercises 3-4 and 3-5 Working with Synthesis

This exercise asks you to attempt a synthesis. Here you will compare two popular reality shows, American Idol *and* The Amazing Race.

The Amazing Race is normally described as a "reality show," the same descriptor as applied to American Idol. *Like the* Idol *series,* The Amazing Race *has had an extended run since 2001 and has earned Emmy Awards and a high audience ranking. The Race is a competition among eleven teams, though there have been either twelve or ten teams on a few occasions. Generally, the teams are provided with an allowance to look after food, lodging, and incidental expenses, and compete with one another to win a particular leg of the race. They are given general route information, faced with obstacles, and assisted by route markers along the way. Each team must try to complete the race in as high a finishing position as it can accomplish. The last team to finish is disqualified from the competition unless it is a non-elimination leg. Once the field has been narrowed to three teams, a final leg is run, and the winning team receives the million-dollar prize.*

Before you begin the work that will prepare you to write a synthesis based on these two shows, please begin by writing a definition of the term "reality show." For additional information on writing a definition, check 8-c-3 and 13-d. Generally, we begin a definition by placing the entity to be defined in its class and then describing its distinctive characteristics. This exercise asks you to think about the distinctive characteristics of "reality shows" before attempting a synthesized view of two sample shows.

Exercise 3-4 Definition

In the space provided, write an extended definition of "reality show." In your definition, include the characteristics of reality shows and indicate which of these apply to the two shows you are going to write about.

DEFINITION: Identify the class to which the term to be defined belongs.

_____
_____
_____
_____
_____
_____
_____
_____
_____
_____

DEFINITION (ctd.): Use contrast to develop your definition.

How does a "reality show" differ from a "fictional show"? Try to think of at least six significant differences. You may number them if you prefer.

_____
_____
_____
_____
_____
_____
_____
_____
_____
_____

DEFINITION (ctd.): Use comparison to develop your definition.

What do you consider the key characteristics of a "reality show"? Try to think of at least six significant characteristics. You may number them if you prefer. Feel free to refer to *The Amazing Race* and *American Idol* to support your choices.

_____
_____
_____
_____
_____
_____
_____
_____
_____
_____
_____

SUMMARY OF DEFINITION

Use the additional space you have to make a list of the key parts of your definition, including the class to which you assigned your term and the characteristics that distinguish it from other members of that class.

1.

2. (etc.)

Exercise 3-5 Creating a Synthesis

Now that you have taken the time to organize a definition of your key term, "reality show," you should be prepared to write a synthesis, one that brings the elements together and applies them in an assessment of how these two particular "reality shows" reveal the essential character of "reality shows," and of the appeal they have, both to their audiences and to their makers.

Part II ACADEMIC WRITING

Chapter 9 Summary

Exercise 9-1 The Summary

As you read the following passage, underline the elements of the passage you think should be in a summary. Once you have selected the material you think is central to a summary of the passage, write a summary using your own words.

In his book *On Equilibrium*, John Ralston Saul comments that people have forgotten to use common sense when dealing with social problems. Instead of dealing with poverty or homelessness by looking at their underlying causes and working to eliminate them, we only examine the data on poverty and homelessness and react to issues when there is a spike in the number of people affected. In other words, we are reactive, not proactive. We react to suppress the dramatic rise of a problem. When the crisis declines, we move on to reacting to other urgent problems that are conspicuously above the norm. As a result, we do not abide by a set of social principles that we believe are fundamental to the rights of every member of society.

Saul suggests we have gone back to mid-nineteenth-century moralism and its views on people in distress. Moralism, according to Saul, reinforces the divisions between the people who hold power and wealth and those who do not. It asserts the right of those in power to feel good about charitable donations for those in misery. This method of helping underprivileged people is reflected in infomercials on television that appeal to viewers to support children in developing countries by making a personal and financial contribution to a child's development. These appeals strengthen their case by noting that people who donate will receive a photograph of the child they are supporting and get progress letters from the child to show how sponsors' donations are helping. The appeal and the support becomes personal, the link between those supporting the charity and the individuals being supported tangible. In this method of funding, those who can afford to help get to feel good about doing so; those who are supported get to thank those who support them, but the underlying problems are not examined, let alone solved.

Sadly, according to Saul, in a world bereft of common sense, more and more individuals become marginalized, and more and more people need food banks and charity to lead, not normal, but impoverished lives. Common sense suggests that, as a society, we should be working to ensure people are not marginalized. We should be examining the underlying problems of poverty and homelessness and working to eliminate them so that we don't have to spend endless amounts of money dealing with outcomes that can be avoided. We should not have to have a part of the population feeling good about its wealth to the point where it feels good about supporting those that society fails, those who cannot afford to live normal lives. Something is dreadfully wrong with society when an elite portion of society feels good about supporting an underprivileged underclass.

The poorest federal riding in Canada, the Vancouver Downtown Eastside, has, for years, presented a problem of abject poverty mixed with drug and alcohol problems. Every year, politicians argue about how to deal with homelessness, alcoholism, drug use, and prostitution in this riding; every year, millions of dollars are spent on projects that do not eliminate the poverty creating these issues, but, instead, treat the symptoms manifested by those trapped in poverty. Can society afford to continue ignoring the plight of such people and still see itself as humane? In his book, Saul remarks, "What common sense provides is a clear sense that nothing is inevitable; that we belong to a society" (64). What Saul is pointing out is that people often forget they are a part of a greater whole rather than isolated from it and its problems.

(588 words)

Source: John Ralston Saul, *On Equilibrium* (Toronto: Viking-Penguin, 2001).

Part III RESEARCH ESSAYS

Chapter 15 Step 3: Conducting Research

Exercise 15-1 Electronic Research Techniques

The following exercise should help you unearth the potential of online sources and the online resources of your library. Your results will depend on how much time you put into such a search. Give yourself some time. Make sure you can use the search elements of each part of this exercise.

Scenario: You are faced with writing an essay on Aboriginal writers of Canada. Your instructor suggests you look at *Me Funny,* the 2006 collection of writing on or by Aboriginal Canadians edited by Drew Hayden Taylor. Your library may not have it in its collection, but you should be able to find it. Similarly, you have been told to look at the third edition of *An Anthology of Canadian Native Literature in English,* edited by Daniel David Moses and Terry Goldie, which was published in 2005 by Oxford University Press Canada. Your instructor has also suggested that you look at books related to the topic, including these:

King, Thomas. *The Truth About Stories: A Native Narrative.* Toronto: Anansi, 2003.

——. *A Short History of Indians in Canada.* Toronto: HarperCollins, 2005.

——. *Green Grass, Running Water.* Toronto: HarperCollins, 1993.

Francis, Daniel. *The Imaginary Indian: The Image of the Indian in Canadian Culture,* Vancouver: Arsenal, 1992.

Stonechild, Blair, and Bill Waiser. *Loyal Till Death: Indians and the North-West Rebellion.* Calgary: Fifth House, 1997.

Boyden, Joseph. *Three Day Road.* Viking Penguin, 2005.

By looking at some of these books and getting a sense of your topic, you will start to gather ideas that will help you shape your topic and choose a direction to take in your paper.

Next, you need to find two online sources for your topic. To do this, you need to find one or two articles related to it. As well, you might try to locate some background information on one or two Native writers you wish to focus on in your paper.

For instance, you might go to your library's online search page and, in the search box *Academic Search Premier*, type "King, Thomas," and in the next search box, "criticism."

Searching: Academic Search Premier   Choose Databases

King, Thomas		In Select a Field (optional)	Search	Clear
and	Criticism	In Select a Field (optional)		

If you do, one of the first items the search engine will generate for you is

1. "Writing, Speaking, and Gender Blending: Reading Greek Allusions in 'Truth and Bright Water.'" Rintoul, Suzanne. *Mosaic: A Journal for the Interdisciplinary Study of Literature*, Sep2007, Vol. 40 Issue 3, p123–137, 15p; (*AN 27358241*)

There will be a link from this listing to the article itself. Next, put terms you want the search page to process, find two articles on a subject relevant to your topic, and write the results in the space provided. You ought to preview the articles to make sure they are relevant. Besides the bibliographic information, you should also jot down a few notes about the article's focus.

1.
_____
_____
_____
_____

2. _____
_____
_____
_____
_____
_____

Using the same search technique, come up with *one general information source* for your topic.

_____
_____
_____
_____
_____

Next, *select one article, story or poem* from either *Me Funny* or *An Anthology of Canadian Native Literature in English* and see if you can come up with information on the author.

Author: _____

Information source: _____
_____

Information: _____
_____
_____

Now that you have used the electronic search tools available in your library, go to Google and *do a simple online search of the author and the topic* to see what you can find on the Internet. The one thing you should notice right away is that you will get a mix of material. Some of it may be good; some of it may not be as reliable as the material you found in your online library search. Below, list two of the items you found in your Google search and comment on whether they are good or marginal sources of material. In doing this search, remember to use Boolean terms and to set terms or phrases off from one another using the techniques suggested to you in Part II, Chapter 15 of your handbook.

1.

_____
_____
_____
_____
_____

2.

_____
_____
_____
_____
_____

Part IV DOCUMENTATION

Chapter 21 Avoiding Plagiarism

Exercise 21-1 Plagiarism: The Essentials

The following exercise will strengthen your sense of what plagiarism is and how to avoid it. For each question, select what you think is the right answer.

1. If I find something on the Web, it is obviously in the public domain, and I don't have to cite my source.

   Correct _____ Wrong _____

2. There is no author listed on the website, so students can cut and paste sentences or even short passages into their essay without showing that they got the material from the Web.

   Correct _____ Wrong _____

3. If I can find the same information in a variety of newspaper, radio, television, and online sources, I don't have to cite where I got the information.

   Correct _____ Wrong _____

4. Two people can work together and share their work and not have to worry about plagiarism.

   Correct _____ Wrong _____

5. Encyclopaedias do not have to be cited either in the text of my essay or my bibliography.

   Correct _____ Wrong _____

6. I have a friend who took the same course last semester. I asked her if I could look at her paper and draw ideas from it. I don't have to worry about plagiarism as she said I could use her paper.

   Correct _____ Wrong _____

7. If I just use a phrase from a website or a book, that is plagiarism.

   Correct _____ Wrong _____

8. If I list the material I have looked at and used in writing my essay in my bibliography, I should still worry about plagiarism.

   Correct _____ Wrong _____

9. The tutor in the learning centre helped strengthen my writing and straighten out some of my ideas, but that is not a problem.

   Correct _____ Wrong _____

10. I cited my quotation on the first page. It is clear that my second quotation (on page four) is from the same source, but I still have to cite my second quotation.

    Correct _____ Wrong _____

11. If I am using a source that generally is relating common knowledge, then specific information that is not necessarily found in three or more sources does not have to be cited.

    Correct _____ Wrong _____

12. A summary does not need to be cited. After all, it is in my own words, not the author's.

    Correct _____ Wrong _____

13. I took notes in class. I am going to use the exact words of my instructor. I should cite him and the date of the class in my essay.

    Correct _____ Wrong _____

14. Wikipedia is jointly authored by people who use the site. As such, there is no author and I don't have to cite any borrowings from the site.

    Correct _____ Wrong _____

Exercise 21-2 Plagiarism: Knowing What to Avoid

The following passage includes issues linked to plagiarism that could result in the assignment receiving a grade of zero for plagiarism. Locate the errors and suggest solutions in the space provided between the lines.

The Sources

Below is a list of the source material used in the paper:

Website: The Complete Works of George Orwell

**Novel title*:* *Coming Up For Air* by George Orwell

http://www.george-orwell.org/Coming_up_for_Air/22.html. Accessed May 5, 2009.

Coming Up For Air, **Part 4, Chapter 6**

War is coming. 1941, they say. And there'll be plenty of broken crockery, and little houses ripped open like packing-cases, and the guts of the chartered accountant's clerk plastered over the piano that he's buying on the never-never. But what does that kind of thing matter, anyway? I'll tell you what my stay in Lower Binfield had taught me, and it was this. IT'S ALL GOING TO HAPPEN. All the things you've got at the back of your mind, the things you're terrified of, the things that you tell yourself are just a nightmare or only happen in foreign countries. The bombs, the food-queues, the rubber truncheons, the barbed wire, the coloured shirts, the slogans, the enormous faces, the machine-guns squirting out of bedroom windows. It's all going to happen. I know it—at any rate, I knew it then. There's no escape. Fight against it if you like, or look the other way and pretend not to notice, or grab your spanner and rush out to do a bit of face-smashing along with the others. But there's no way out. It's just something that's got to happen. (No page numbers in the online text)

Website: wikipedia.org

Title of page: George Orwell

http://en.wikipedia.org/wiki/George_Orwell. Accessed May 1, 2009.

"Another bombshell was Cape's withdrawal of support of *Animal Farm*. The decision is believed to be due to the influence of Peter Smollett, who worked at the Ministry of Information and was later disclosed to be a Soviet agent.[30]"

"30. Timothy Garton Ash: "Orwell's List" in *The New York Review of Books*, Number 14, 25 September 2003." [http://www.nybooks.com/articles/16550]

Related website to the above:

Timothy Garton Ash: "Orwell's List" in *The New York Review of Books*, 25 September 2003. http://www.nybooks.com/articles/16550. Accessed May 5, 2009.

"Peter Smollett," Orwell noted: "... gives strong impression of being ... [a] Russian agent." Smollett was the head of the Soviet section in the British Ministry of Information ... [and] a Soviet agent ... Second, he was almost certainly the official on whose advice the publisher Jonathan Cape turned down *Animal Farm* as an unhealthily anti-Soviet text.

Website: wikipedia.org

Title of page: Animal Farm

http://en.wikipedia.org/wiki/Animal_Farm. Accessed May 1, 2009.

"Orwell, a democratic socialist and a member of the Independent Labour Party for many years, was a critic of Joseph Stalin and was suspicious of Moscow-directed Stalinism after his experiences with the NKVD during the Spanish Civil War."

Website: wikipedia.org

Title of the page: Nuremberg Defense

http://en.wikipedia.org/wiki/Nuremberg_Defense. Accessed May 5, 2009.

"The Nuremberg Defense is a legal defense that ... the defendant was 'only following orders' ... and is therefore not responsible for his crimes ...

"This defense is still used often ... that an unlawful order presents a dilemma from which there is no legal escape. One who refuses an unlawful order will still probably be jailed for refusing orders, and one who accepts one will probably be jailed for committing unlawful acts."

Online journal article:

Orwell's "Marrakech." By: March, Thomas, *Explicator*, 00144940, Spring99, Vol. 57, Issue 3 p. 163-164. Database: Academic Search Premier. Accessed May 3, 2009

"*Marrakech*" is a morality play, and *Orwell* ... forces us to see as he has seen, to react with his own moral indignation. We experience along with him the disgust, terror, and pity of realizing that the bumps in the path ... are really disregarded human remains. (p. 163)

Online journal article:

"Lies, Damned Lies and Literature: George Orwell and 'The Truth'." By: Ingle, Stephen. *British Journal of Politics & International Relations*, Nov 2007, Vol. 9 Issue 4, p730-746, 17p; Database: Academic Search Premier. Accessed May 3, 2009.

Nineteen Eighty-Four:

"Its basic premise appears at first glance to be that the only possible constraint upon a totalitarian regime is provided by the individual acting as an autonomous moral agent capable of passing judgements upon the nature of external reality." (733)

The passage:

George Orwell and the Politics of the Mid-Twentieth Century

Many postsecondary students have read either George Orwell's *Animal Farm* or *1984* in high school and understand that, in these books, Orwell was criticizing the state of Europe in the period immediately following WW II. But Orwell's writing had its roots in the fact that he was a democratic socialist, a member of the Independent Labour Party, and both strongly critical of the leadership of Joseph Stalin and suspicious of Moscow-directed Stalinism. It shouldn't be surprising that Orwell's *Animal Farm* did not come into print without some problems. Its publication history is curiously affected by the politics Orwell was critical of. The book's original publisher, Jonathan Cape, backed out of publishing Orwell's book due to the influence of Peter Smollett, who worked at the Ministry of Information. Smollett, it later turned out, was spying for the USSR and obviously did not want Orwell's book, which he felt was critical of the Soviet Union, to be published. It was one year after the planned publication date that another publisher finally published *Animal Farm*.

Orwell's critical view of dictatorial states is again in evidence in *1984*, where Orwell advises his readers that the only possible constraint upon a totalitarian regime arises when an individual passes judgements upon the nature of external reality. Orwell is aware that individuals are ultimately responsible for regimes. He holds the position that there is no neutral ground. A non-response condones the acts of a regime just as much as willing participation in the acts of a regime. No one can hold a neutral ground; everyone is responsible for the acts of the state and for tyranny. Even though Orwell took the position that there is no such thing as a neutral stance in a tyrannical society, it is easy to see that people in such societies could feel they were faced with a dilemma from which there is no legal escape. They would be damned by their society if they did not follow orders, and damned by others if they followed orders and took part in an atrocity against a group of people.

Orwell's criticism of the middle of the twentieth century dates back to the period before WWII, as his novel *Coming Up For Air,* which was first published in June 1939, three months before Britain's declaration of war in September 1939, demonstrates. In that novel, Orwell's narrator foresees a horrific future:

> All the things you've got at the back of your mind, the things you're terrified of, the things that you tell yourself are just a nightmare or only happen in foreign countries. The bombs, the food-queues, the rubber truncheons, the barbed wire, the coloured shirts, the slogans, the enormous faces, the machine-guns squirting out of bedroom windows. It's all going to happen.

Coming Up For Air was not the only work that Orwell published in 1939 that warned of impending war and social chaos. His essay "Marrakech" not only foresees the cataclysm of war on the horizon but also points to underlying causes of many of the conflicts that would create social discord in the world for the next fifty years. At the end of his essay, while observing a column of Senegalese French Army soldiers marching past, he asks the question "How much longer can we go on kidding these people? How long before they turn their guns in the other direction?" (234). Here, not only is Orwell seeing the movement toward world war, but he is also making his readers aware of the problems that lurk just below the surface of the colonial empires that had developed in the nineteenth century. In fact, "Marrakech" is a morality play, and *Orwell* forces us to see the poverty and problems of colonial empires and feel his moral indignation.

Works Cited

Ingle, Stephen. "Lies, Damned Lies and Literature: George Orwell and 'The Truth'." *British Journal of Politics & International Relations*, 9.4 (2007): 730-746. Academic Search Premier. Web. 3 May 2009.

Orwell, George. *Coming Up for Air*. *The Complete Works of George Orwell*. n. pag. Web. 5 May 2009.

———. "Marrakech." *The Nelson Introduction to Literature*. Ed. Al Valleau and Jack Finnbogason. Toronto: Nelson, 2004. 230–234.

Chapters 22–25 MLA, APA, Chicago, and Columbia Online Styles

Exercise 22-1 MLA, APA, Chicago, and Columbia Online Styles

The following exercise is meant to test whether you understand some of the distinct elements of the current MLA, APA, Chicago, and Columbia Online styles. As well, some of the questions test your ability to deal with how each style deals with online material. If, after completing the exercise, you feel you need to review one of the styles, please reread Chapters 22 to 25 as needed.

1. Which of the following entries reflects the current MLA style for a works cited entry?

   a) Finnbogason, Jack and Al Valleau. A Canadian Writer's Guide. 4th ed. Toronto: Nelson, 2009.

   b) Finnbogason, Jack and Al Valleau. *A Canadian Writer's Guide*. 4th ed. Toronto: Nelson, 2009. Print.

   c) Finnbogason, Jack and Al Valleau. *A Canadian Writer's Guide*. 4th ed. Toronto: Nelson, 2009.

2. Which of the following entries reflects the current MLA style for a works cited entry?

   a) March, Thomas. "Orwell's 'Marrakech.'" *Explicator*, 57.3 (1999): 163-64. Web. 3 May 2009.

   b) March, Thomas. "Orwell's 'Marrakech.'" *Explicator*, 57.3 (1999): 163-64. *Academic Search Premier*. 3 May 2009.

   c) March, Thomas. "Orwell's 'Marrakech.'" *Explicator*, 57.3 (1999): 163-64. *Academic Search Premier*. Web.

   d) March, Thomas. "Orwell's 'Marrakech.'" *Explicator*, 57.3 (1999): 163-64. *Academic Search Premier*. Web. 3 May 2009.

3. In the seventh edition of the *MLA Handbook*, titles of books are

    a)   underlined.

    b)   placed in quotation marks.

    c)   italicized.

4. The 2009 edition of the *MLA Handbook* says that if your online source does not include page numbers,

    a) you count the paragraphs and cite the paragraph number in your in-text reference.

    b) you use 1 for the first page of the article, number the pages of the article, and use the number that corresponds to the page your quotation is on for an in-text citation.

    c) you make a reference to the author, or, if there is no author, the title of the work, in your in-text reference.

    d) you introduce the author's name or the work's name in the lead-in to your quotation.

    e) either c or d is correct.

5. In APA style, if you are using an electronic version of an article available in print, add, in brackets, after the title of the article, the word(s)

    a) Web.

    b) Online.

    c) Electronic Version.

6. In APA style, when you cite electronic work, after you have indicated the date you accessed the material, you

    a)   add the word "Web" to the end of the reference.

    b)   add the URL without making any breaks in the URL.

    c)   add the URL, breaking the URL after a period or a slash.

7. In APA style, titles of books and periodicals are

   a) underlined.

   b) italicized.

   c) placed in quotation marks.

8. In Chicago style, when you cite online sources, the date of access is indicated at the end of your citation in the following style:

   a) Accessed 4 June 2009.

   b) (accessed June 4, 2009).

   c) Retrieved June 4 2009.

9. In Chicago style, titles of books are

   a) italicized

   b) placed in quotation marks

   c) underlined

10. In Chicago style, before the date of access, online references are indicated by

    a) adding the word "Web."

    b) adding a URL, making breaks between any punctuation or slash if necessary.

    c) adding a URL, making breaks after a slash if necessary.

11. In Chicago style,

    a) access date is indicated after the URL in a citation by adding "Accessed 4 June, 2009."

    b) access date is indicated before the URL in a citation by adding "Accessed June 4, 2009."

    c) access date is not indicated in a citation unless the data is time-sensitive or the resource is not stable.

    d) the date of access is indicated by adding "(accessed June 4, 2009)" after the URL.

    e) Both c and d are correct.

    f) Both b and c are correct.

Chapters 22–25 *MLA, APA, Chicago, and Columbia Online Styles*   49

12. In Columbia Online style, the references or works cited at the end of the essay are

   a) single-spaced whether the essay is being submitted electronically or in print.

   b) single-spaced in electronic submissions and double-spaced in print submissions.

   c) double-spaced in both electronic and print submissions, but electronic submissions do not indent any of the lines of the entries, and they place two blank lines between each entry.

   d) double-spaced in both electronic and print submissions.

13. In Columbia Online style, the date of access

   a) is never indicated.

   b) is indicated at the end of the entry by adding (accessed 4 June 2009).

   c) is indicated at the end of the entry by adding (4 June 2009).

14. Columbia Online style suggests that entries for a Blog/Chat/Moo be presented with

   a) the name of the Blog/Chat/Moo added after the author's name, the title, and the date of the posting.

   b) the name of the Blog/Chat/Moo added just before the URL.

   c) the name of the Blog/Chat/Moo added right after the author's name and the title of the entry.

Part V BASIC GRAMMAR

Chapter 27 Parts of Speech

Exercise 27-1 Identifying Parts of Speech

1. Identify the nouns, pronouns, verbs, and adverbs in the following sentences. Place the correct number above each word in the sentence that corresponds to the following code: **1 = noun, 2 = pronoun, 3 = verb**, and **4 = adverb**.

    a) Many problems associated with the production and distribution of food have recently been recognized.

    b) One of the largest issues is the volume of water required to produce food.

    c) For instance, it takes four pounds of water to produce one pound of beef.

    d) A pound of grain, however, can be grown with only one pound of water.

    e) If we all consumed grain as our principal food, we would quickly reduce the amount of water we need.

    f) However, the direction that food production is taking is the opposite of what is needed.

    g) As large new middle classes are created in countries like India and China, the demand for meat increases.

    h) People who have a larger income feel they are entitled to increase the amount of meat in their diet.

    i) If we had an unending supply of water, this shift would not be a problem.

    j) But the fact is that we are rapidly depleting our water supply in North America and elsewhere.

2. In each of the following sentences, identify the adjectives, adverbs, conjunctions, prepositions, and articles by placing the appropriate number above the word using the following code: **1 = adjective, 2 = adverb, 3 = conjunction, 4 = preposition,** and **5 = article**.

   a) A second aspect of the rise in food prices on a worldwide basis is the shifting value of corn.

   b) Where corn was once grown principally for food, whether it was eaten by livestock or humans, it is increasingly grown as an alternative source of fuel for vehicles.

   c) The American Midwest was once a major supplier of food for humans.

   d) Now, more and more land is set aside to grow corn as a biofuel, a cheap alternative for oil.

   e) On the surface, such a change might seem to be a prudent decision.

   f) However, an unintended result is the increase of the value of land now that it can produce an alternative to oil costing a hundred dollars a barrel or more.

   g) As the land's cost increases, the farmer is reluctant to devote it to growing cattle corn.

   h) This means a rise in the cost of beef and other livestock, one of the staple foods consumed in North America.

   i) We also know now that the energy necessary to convert corn to ethanol, a fuel, is significant, so the contribution to reducing our dependency on oil is not as great as we had hoped it would be.

j) As in other matters, we learn that an apparently simple cause turns out to be complex, and the wish to do a good thing about our energy use creates more harm than we had anticipated.

3. In each of the following sentences, identify the nouns, pronouns, verbs, adjectives, adverbs, conjunctions, and prepositions by placing the appropriate number above the word using the following code: **1 = noun, 2 = pronoun, 3 = verb, 4 = adjective, 5 = adverb, 6 = conjunction,** and **7 = preposition**.

a) The costs of energy are a hidden but major contributor to the cost of food in all major areas of the world, whether that food be grain or rice, beef or fish.

b) When the price of oil increases by 50% in the space of six months, the world's food markets are affected.

c) The fuel used by tractors to plough the earth, by trucks, ships, and trains to deliver food to market, becomes a much larger cost to the producer and consumer.

d) The end result is that a worldwide food crisis is created.

e) If you add in the effect of a tragic typhoon in Burma/Myanmar, then a particular market like rice is doubly affected.

f) The rice bowl of Asia, Burma/Myanmar and Vietnam, have both suffered major rice crop failures that will create a shortage of a staple Asian food and raise prices.

g) Unfortunately, this form of price inflation in food costs comes at a time when the world economy has suffered a decline because of mortgage collapses in the United States and the threat of recession elsewhere.

h) This kind of development reminds us of how intricately the world's markets are linked.

i) The escalation of prices for wheat, rice, corn, beef, and pork caused by nature and by humans hurts most of us eventually.

j) If we, at the same time, are struggling to pay off or qualify for a mortgage, the pain we feel will be intensified.

Chapter 28 Phrases and Clauses

Exercise 28-1 Prepositional Phrases

The following passage includes a number of prepositional phrases. Underline the phrases and indicate, using the key below, whether they are acting as adjectives, adverbs, or subjects.

   Adjective = adj

   Adverb = adv

   Subject = s

For most Canadians, a trip across Canada is one of the essential ways of coming to terms with the complexity of the country and its people. Canada is a broad, vast land, and it is composed of distinct regions that have distinct cultures with different attitudes. It would be wrong to make a generalization about the people of Canada, despite what politicians would like Canadians to think. From the east coast of Canada in Newfoundland, to the west coast of British Columbia, Canada's geography and people, although united by common laws and common purposes, are distinctly different from one another. Talking to a Newfoundlander in St. John's and a British Columbian in Victoria will illustrate the differences in Canadians. Both people live on one of Canada's coasts, but, the minute they open their mouths, the differences are evident. Not only are the accents startlingly different, but the concerns are different as well. How people view their country as a whole may be similar, but, across the country, local cultures may vary considerably. In a journey traversing the country lies knowledge. In the end, we only become familiar with the complexity of our country by experiencing its different regions.

30 prepositional phrases in total

Exercise 28-2 Participial, Gerundial, and Infinitive Phrases

The following passage includes participial, gerundial, and infinitive phrases. Underline and identify whether they are participial, gerundial, or infinitive, and indicate whether the phrases are acting as adjectives, adverbs, or nouns.

P = participial   adjective = 1

G = Gerundial   adverb = 2

I = Infinitive   noun = 3

Crossing the country by car is one way to notice the geographical and cultural differences of the country. Touring by car has become a vacation pastime in North America, and it certainly is one of the major ways that Canadians come to appreciate the different parts of their country. To see Niagara Falls is to experience its enormity. Seeing the Rocky Mountains in the distance from Calgary, we can understand the sharp contrast they make with the western Canadian prairies. Gone are the days when people on one coast never saw the other coast or the land in between. Now the outstanding sights of every region are a part of every Canadian's perspective on his or her country. Walking the streets of Victoria's Chinatown, people will quickly realize they are in the midst of the oldest Chinese community in the country. Seeing the old buildings is, in itself, a treat, but the old buildings allow us to visualize the complex history of the community. Seeing our history and understanding its complexity permit us to appreciate the diversity of the communities that comprise the Canadian cultural complex.

14 items to classify

Exercise 28-3 Appositive and Absolute Phrases

Identify the appositive and absolute phrases in the following passage by underlining each of them and placing "Ap" above the appositives and "Ab" above each absolute. Circle the word or words the appositives identify or describe.

Your ticket firmly grasped in your hand, you are off to an NHL hockey game. What can you expect from your experience in an era when there are almost five times as many teams as there were fifty years ago? Your local team, the team that plays closest to where you live, will often have a large following if you live in Canada. For instance, the Toronto Maple Leafs, the team of southern Ontario, have a fan base that is so large that it is almost impossible to get tickets to a game. It is not uncommon to hear stories about long-time fans, ticket holders who inherited tickets that have been in the family for more than thirty years. These fans, the ones who have been loyal to a team that has not won the Stanley Cup since 1967, deserve better.

    Of course, the difficulty in purchasing tickets to games in some Canadian markets is compounded by ticket resellers. The face price for an inexpensive ticket may be $35, but the resale price, the price you will have to pay for a ticket that someone is reselling, may be $100. I have even heard season ticket holders boast that they can sell some of their tickets, go to select games, and do so at no cost at all because of the profit they make from reselling the tickets. Thus, the tickets priced by the hockey team for families, the ones usually in the top of the arena, no longer make for an inexpensive night out.

    Yet the story of the NHL fan does not end with the story of the long-time season ticket holder or the price of tickets. A close look at the individual fan tells another story. Her money paid out for tickets, the keen hockey fan now has only to think about the cost

Chapter 28 *Phrases and Clauses* **57**

of food, drink, and souvenirs, which have become a part of the game experience. A simple baseball cap, one with the team's logo on it, can cost between $25 to $30, and this is one of the least expensive souvenirs. A game jersey, one with a player's name and number on it, can cost over $300. Think how sad it can be can be. Her banner waving while proudly wearing her newly purchased player jersey, the avid hockey fan approaches the stadium, ticket in hand, only to find out that her favourite player has been traded that morning for "future considerations."

11 phrases in total

Exercise 28-4 All Phrase Types

The following passage includes a number of phrases. Underline the phrases and indicate whether they are verb (V), participial (Part), gerundial (G), infinitive (I), appositive (Ap), absolute (Ab), or prepositional (P).

Local governments, the people who really make decisions, need to be serious about transportation if they really want drastic changes to occur in people's commuting habits. Adding a few new buses in the urban centres will do nothing to eliminate the problems that people in the suburban regions across the country face in moving from one place to another to work or go to school. Why do governments considering this transportation problem continue to support the building of new roadways and large malls on the edges of suburban sprawl rather than planning a better sustainable urban infrastructure and mass transportation system? It is never going to get inexpensive to build an extensive system. Going slowly will not solve the problem. Commuting, moving across town to work, is only going to become easier if the city puts money and energy into mass transportation. Politicians, their political careers at stake, may well understand that voters are concerned, but they may lack the will to make broad changes that will make a real difference in the way people think about moving from one place to another. To understand the complexity of transportation, politicians have to think beyond what modes of transportation are being used currently. Planning for the future, thinking beyond tomorrow, is not easy work. Nor does it mean thinking of simply expanding what we have. Their biases discarded, politicians have to consider how best to deal with urban sprawl. Suffering the irritant of poor transportation systems, voters may not tolerate political incompetence much longer.

48 phrases in total

Exercise 28-5 Constructing Phrases

The following exercise will give you a chance to test whether you understand how to construct different types of phrases. In each sentence, using the type of phrase in the brackets, construct a phrase that will work with the rest of the sentence.

1. Down [prepositional phrase] _____ lay the golf ball.

2. I wanted [infinitive phrase] _____ if I could strike the ball where it lay.

3. [participial phrase] _____ , I noticed that there was a rock right in front of it.

4. [gerundial phrase] _____ onto the fairway was not going to be easy.

5. I was going [infinitive phrase] _____ if I could accomplish the task.

6. [appositive phrase] Gordon, _____ , came over to see my plight.

7. [absolute phrase] _____ , he suggested I take a penalty stroke and move the ball.

8. After all, he reasoned, a ball [restrictive appositive phrase] _____ would be much easier to hit than what faced me in the rough.

9. [participial phrase] _____ , I quickly saw he was right.

10. [gerundial phrase] _____ was the correct course of action. I picked up the ball and dropped it on the fairway where I could hit it without fear of having it bounce right back at me.

60 Part V *Basic Grammar*

Exercise 28-6 Adding Phrases to Clauses

The following exercise gives you practice in building sentences through the addition of phrases. You are asked to add the type of phrase indicated to increase the content of the sentence it joins.

1. The 2008 financial crisis, [appositive phrase] _____

   _____ , generated pain

   for Americans first and for the rest of the world next.

2. Wall Street, [prepositional phrase] _____

   _____ , was seen as the

   culprit, but we quickly learned that the American government was also at fault.

3. The Canadian banking authorities began [infinitive phrase] _____

   _____ when it became

   clear that their restrictions on approving mortgages were prudent checks.

4. [absolute phrase] _____ ,

   the American public couldn't believe that financial experts could create a mess

   that wound up killing their own companies.

5. Canadian investors, [participial phrase] _____

   _____ , soon discovered that all but one

   Canadian bank had heavy investments in American sub-prime mortgage funds.

6. [prepositional phrase] _____ , however, our banks had the resources to overcome the losses caused by the sub-prime mortgage collapse.

7. [gerund phrase] _____ , it appears, takes as much skill as being a prudent banker.

8. The bubble payment, [appositive phrase] _____ _____ , was the first factor to cause people to walk away from their sub-prime mortgages and initiate the financial collapse of some major American financial institutions.

9. [absolute phrase] _____ , President Bush was forced to appeal to Congress to approve a bailout of the American financial industry.

10. Ironically, [prepositional phrase] _____ _____ , the world was treated to the spectacle of government rescuing the financial industry from a collapse fuelled primarily by greed.

Exercise 28-7 Clauses

The following passage includes a number of sentences that have more than one clause. Circle the independent clauses and underline the dependent clauses in each sentence. If the clauses are dependent, indicate whether they are adverbial, adjectival, or noun clauses.

The problem most students have composing an essay is they do not have a thesis or major claim that is well formed. Unless they learn to limit their focus, they will find their task very difficult. When students start to write an essay, they can become overwhelmed by the task. Unless they utilize prewriting strategies, they may even find it hard to develop a well-formed topic with a clear thesis. The best beginning strategy is to write down all the points relative to the topic. Then the task becomes easier, for it is an easy step from a list of relevant points to using a mind-map, free-writing, or applying the Pentad to focus the topic and isolate a thesis. Once they have done that, they can then consider how to further organize their material. Although a formal outline is often the next step that students take in the writing process, they should first consider what points they have gathered that are most central to their argument and to the length of their paper. These are essential factors to take into account. If students neglect to narrow their topic in this way, they may find they are spending a considerable amount of time working on material they will eventually have to cut.

Part VI SENTENCE ELEMENTS

Chapter 29 Parts of Sentences

Exercise 29-1 Identifying Parts of Sentences—Subjects

Underline the complete subjects in the following sentences and circle the simple subjects.

1. In 2008, one female leader and four male leaders led their parties in the election to determine Canada's next government.

2. Most commentators agreed that, in the televised October debate among those leaders, the head of the Green Party was the most aggressive in advancing her ideas and attacking the ideas of her competitors.

3. In one of the debate's liveliest exchanges, she lectured Stephen Harper, the sitting prime minister, on his shortcomings.

4. Intriguingly, that same night, on American television, Senator Joe Biden, vice-presidential nominee of the Democratic Party, and Governor Sarah Palin, vice-presidential nominee of the Republican Party, debated their parties' respective positions.

5. In the newspapers the next day, the survey of audience response showed our preference for Biden and Palin over Dion, Duceppe, Harper, Layton, and May.

6. Though an unexpected result, we should recognize that our preferring the American debate over the Canadian debate is understandable.

7. Most of us were more focused on American candidates than on Canadian ones because of their novelty.

8. Why would the average Canadian be startled to learn of the novelty of Biden and Palin over people appearing on our television news repeatedly?

9. Isn't novelty the principal quality the Canadian viewer of television seeks?

10. Therefore, May, Biden, and Palin proved to be more interesting characters to Canadian viewers than Harper, Layton, Duceppe, and Dion.

Exercise 29-2 Identifying Parts of Sentences—Clauses

In the following exercise, underline and identify the following parts of each clause:

Clause subject = circle

Clause predicate = underlined

Remember that a dependent clause may be a part of an independent clause and be embedded in it. So there may be cases where the subject of a dependent clause is in the predicate of an independent clause and is both circled and underlined.

1. Over the past decade, newspaper columnists and television commentators have remarked that young adults have been voting less and less frequently and that those who do vote are the children of parents who vote.

2. Recently, Rick Mercer, in his CBC program, pointed out that, during elections, politicians make sure they visit seniors' homes. Seniors always vote, and the politicians pay attention to seniors' concerns because they vote.

3. On the other hand, he observed that politicians don't seem to be as concerned about attending all-candidates meetings on campuses across Canada. Young people frequently don't exercise their right to vote.

4. He noted that if young people started voting en masse, politicians would make young Canadians' concerns a part of their political party's election platforms.

5. This proves the old adage that the squeaky wheel gets the grease, and the track record of politicians is something young Canadians should pay attention to at election time.

6. Politicians are not concerned about what the people who don't vote are thinking; they are only concerned about what the people who do vote think.

7. If you want to have an effect on how your government is acting, you have to be active and vote.

8. If you don't vote, you can only blame yourself when the government is not doing what you want.

9. Next time you are tempted to say politicians are boring, remember that they do have an effect on your life.

10. They and the legislation they pass may affect your future.

Exercise 29-3 Direct Objects, Indirect Objects, Subject Complements, and Object Complements

In the following exercise, underline and identify the following parts of sentences:

Direct object = DO
Indirect object= IO
Subject complement = SC
Object complement = OC

1. When hockey season starts in the fall, every city and town across the country feels optimistic about its hockey club.

2. Newspaper writers watch the members of their team at training camp and write stories about how fresh and excited all the players look.

3. It is a time of optimism.

4. Neither fans nor reporters are assessing the team realistically.

5. When the puck drops in the first pre-season game, the columnists' attention becomes acute.

6. The new players attack the puck and show the coaching staff their speed and skill.

7. To some, the pre-season is the proving ground.

8. At the end of the pre-season, the coaching staff cut players not performing at the NHL level.

9. The players know the coach's decisions are important.

10. Not surprisingly, the coaches make the players with potential their priority.

Chapter 30 Sentence Patterns

Exercise 30-1 Identifying Sentence Patterns

By placing the number of the relevant sentence pattern at the end of each sentence, identify which of the sentence patterns each sentence follows.

1. *Subject–verb*
2. *Subject–verb–subject complement*
3. *Subject–verb–direct object*
4. *Subject–verb–indirect object–direct object*
5. *Subject–verb–direct object–object complement*

1. Today, job opportunities are changing quickly.

2. It is hard for students to find a career path.

3. People starting off in a career want an interesting, secure job.

4. Yet gone are the days of the one-job career.

5. A secure career is a challenge to find.

6. Students must examine each potential career carefully.

7. Careers change.

8. Advisers must tell students the truth.

9. Students must be vigilant.

10. They do not see their education an unmitigated disaster or a waste of time and money.

11. Their parents may have loaned them money to enable them to complete their education.

12. The axiom "education for an education's sake" is not appropriate anymore.

13. To get an education, many students incur a large debt.

14. The country needs a well-educated youth to ensure the future welfare of the country.

15. Governments should supply students an opportunity to acquire a career.

16. But that career should give them the opportunity to earn a living as well as benefit their country.

17. In elections, ["you" understood] vote for those who support these values.

Chapter 31 Identifying Sentence Types

Exercise 31-1

In the following passage, identify whether a sentence is a simple sentence (S), a compound sentence (C), a complex sentence (Cx), or a compound-complex sentence (CC) by placing the correct abbreviation in the space at the beginning of each sentence.

____ What is it most students look for in a postsecondary institution? ____ Every year, *Maclean's* magazine publishes an issue that lists the "best schools" in Canada, a list that ranks institutions from coast to coast. ____ The magazine advertises its survey will help students find the universities that have the best students, the best professors, the best food, and the best loans and scholarships. ____ Yet is the survey that *Maclean's* has published annually since 1990 of much use, and do students actually use it? ____ When examining the survey, readers need to ask how comprehensive a survey it is when it does not include reviews of a large number of postsecondary institutions in Canada.

____ When many students make the decision to follow a postsecondary course of studies, they consider a number of elements. ____ They consider how close to home the institution is, and they consider what programs the institution offers. ____ They will, of course, take their peers' opinions into consideration when making their decision. ____ These considerations may be tempered by a number of other factors. ____ The cost of the education may be of paramount concern to the student. ____ If the student has good grades in high school and can win a scholarship, tuition fees may not be as strong a concern as they would be for a student who does not have a high GPA.

____ One of the factors related to students' postsecondary studies is tied to whether or not they are taking a full course load or studying part-time. ____ This fact alone is worthy of study. ____ Why would a student want to prolong his or her studies for a degree from four years to eight? ____ A quick survey might reveal that students often cannot afford to go to college or university full-time because of finances; it might also reveal that a large percentage of students are working part-time at low-paying jobs to make their studies possible. ____ To add to their troubles, students who arrive on campuses across Canada for the first time are not always sure what course of studies they want to follow, and they are not necessarily aware of their own strengths and weaknesses. ____ A large number of students who want to be doctors are unaware of the qualities and educational abilities they must possess to be a successful medical school candidate.

____ Students often do not know what they want to do with their education. ____ They do know that the type of service job they will get with only a high school education will pay poorly. ____ Whether or not they consider the numerous opportunities that postsecondary education has to offer them is an interesting question. ____ If they were to read the *Maclean's* review, they might ignore fields of study where they could be happy and gainfully employed. ____ There are careers in the trades and technologies that are interesting and lucrative. ____ *Maclean's* falls short of its duty to publish information that is helpful for all Canadians looking for an education, and it falls short in ways that could easily be rectified if the magazine took a more comprehensive view of education. ____ If it did take these limitations into consideration, it might create an analysis that was meaningful to a broader range of Canadians. ____ That would benefit young Canadians, and it would also benefit *Maclean's*.

Chapter 33 Sentence Variety

Exercise 33-1 Editing Sentences for Variety

Please edit the following paragraph to improve the variety of its sentences. You should be able to reduce the number of sentences by at least half.

One interesting element in the cost of gas is the profit level of gas stations. We read about the eleven billion dollars' profit made by one oil company. That company was Exxon. It made that profit in the first quarter of 2008. That profit level was the largest recorded in the past year. It was, in fact, larger than any profit level ever declared for a quarter. Two quarters later, Exxon declared a quarterly profit of fourteen billion dollars. No company in the history of capitalism ever made so much money in so short a time. We tend to believe that gas stations share in this large profit. We believe that because there are stations carrying the names of Shell and Petro-Canada. However, it is not true. The profit levels of stations attached to oil companies aren't readily available. However, independent stations are not doing well. We know that because they have a national association. It is called the Canadian Independent Petroleum Marketers Association. It pointed out that these stations only have a margin of four to six cents on each litre they sell. The problem they face is compounded by the fact that most buyers of gas use credit cards. The station pays up to two cents per litre per transaction to the credit card company when the customer uses a card. They have to buy their gas on the open market. They also face the decline in driving that has occurred. That decline was a result of rocketing gas prices. The overall effect is one of selling less gas. And, even if oil prices fall, the same basic competitive problem will continue. These problems are compounded by the small profit margin on each sale. Therefore, the independent gas station is struggling. Many have had to close. We cannot be happy about that.

25 sentences total length

Data from Aleksandar Zivojinovic, "Why the Real 'Corner Gas' Is in Trouble," *Maclean's,* July 28, 2008, p. 39.

Exercise 33-2 Editing Sentences for Variety

Please edit the following paragraph to improve the variety of its sentences. You should be able to reduce the number of sentences in the paragraph by at least half.

A major development in the fall of 2008 was a far-reaching financial collapse. This collapse began in the United States. It spread to Europe. It reached as far as Australia and New Zealand. It also affected the stock markets in Hong Kong and Japan. Virtually no market in the world was immune from its effects. Within one week, the American stock market lost 18 percent of its value. The European markets lost 22 percent of their value. Japan saw a plunge of twenty-four per cent in its central stock market. The astounding element to remember is the reason why this happened. It began with a collapse in the value of American real estate. That collapse was caused by house owners walking away from their mortgages. They forfeited their houses because they couldn't pay their mortgage. The rapid escalation in the buying of homes in America happened between 2002 and 2005. It was fuelled by banks and other lending agencies giving mortgages to people who couldn't handle them. Most of these mortgages had a large catch-up payment written into the third year of the mortgage. This was made necessary by the central feature of these mortgages. The payment level granted by lenders to mortgagees was too low to pay for the mortgage. That level was necessary. Without it, the lenders couldn't qualify for a house. The companies who advanced the money to customers then bundled these mortgages into packages. They sold these packages to banks and other financial agencies. In the third year of the mortgages, the house owners encountered the catch-up payment. They started missing payments. Then the financial house had to foreclose. But there were no new buyers. So the value of the houses fell. As it kept falling, foreclosures escalated. So did the decline in housing values. And the financial houses holding the mortgages, in one form or another, had huge debts. They had no resources to pay these debts. The whole empty shell of credit debt collapsed. The financial disaster spread from one stock market to another. It started with the bankruptcy of financial agencies. But it didn't stop there.

(length equals 35 sentences)

Part VIII GRAMMATICAL SENTENCES

Chapter 41 Construction

Exercise 41-1

Correct any fused sentences or comma splices in the sentences that follow. Write the corrected version in the space provided below each sentence. If the sentence is correct, simply write "C" in the space provided.

1. One interesting dimension of the financial recession that started in 2008 was the decline of an American car industry they faced bankruptcy by the end of the year.

2. Despite the fact that GM was the largest company in the world less than ten years ago, it is now facing bankruptcy.

3. Ford is thinking of selling its majority share of Volvo stock, the company believes it will need the money that generates to avoid bankruptcy in the first half of 2009.

4. Not long ago, Chrysler was in serious talks with GM to determine if GM could take over the Chrysler company, alternatively, it wanted to explore with GM the possibility of becoming a junior partner.

_____
_____
_____

5. During 2008, Toyota became the largest seller of cars and trucks in the United States, displacing GM from its traditional occupancy of that position.

_____
_____
_____

6. Perhaps no other statistic is so telling as the actual price of a share of General Motors stock by the latter months of 2008, that share had fallen to a rate equalling its value in 1950.

_____
_____
_____

7. Observers look for simple reasons to explain the decline in the value and solvency of large American car manufacturers, the chief reason is that they ceased making what North Americans wanted.

_____
_____
_____

78 Part VIII *Grammatical Sentences*

8. That reason alone, however, would not have led to the virtual collapse of the largest business in America; there had to be other contributing causes.

_____
_____
_____
_____

9. Perhaps the most important of those subsidiary causes was the fact that it cost American carmakers more to make a car their competitors could build a plant in America and produce cars more cheaply.

_____
_____
_____
_____

10. Ironically, one of the key reasons American carmakers lost the battle for market supremacy was a very simple fact their traditional customers turned to foreign imports.

_____
_____
_____
_____

Exercise 41-2 Recognizing Fragments [I]

In the following exercise you will find a number of fragments. When you locate a fragment, make it into a complete sentence by joining it to the sentence that precedes it or the one that follows it, or by adding the sentence elements necessary to make it a complete sentence. Use the space after each sentence to make the changes you think are necessary.

1. As more and more Canadians live in urban centres, it is easy to forget that, at the beginning of the last century, most of Canada's population lived in small towns or in the countryside.

2. Sadly enough. We have become less and less aware of our rural heritage.

3. Yet small communities still have an impact on the way we see the country and what we value as Canadians.

4. Driving through the countryside, Canada.

80   Part VIII   *Grammatical Sentences*

5. The small villages in photographs, the vistas of what seem to be endless prairies.

6. Those are defining images that we see again and again in photographic essays on the country.

7. Moose in lakes, and prairie dogs beside the road on hind legs.

8. Images like these typify Canada.

9. Just as do, in contrast, pictures of Vancouver and Victoria's historic Chinatowns.

10. However, we are just as likely to identify with the image of the rolling Alberta foothills with cattle spread out across them as we are to an image of a cowboy at the Calgary Stampede.

11. But do Canadians recognize images of the Williams Lake Rodeo?

12. Peggy's Cove?

13. The mouth of the Saguenay River?

14. Even though we may not recognize photographs of all of these places, we proud of our land.

15. And recognize that it has a varied landscape and people.

16. Images that define who we are as much as where we live.

17. Urban images and ones of people, too.

18. St. John's, Halifax, Montreal, Toronto, Winnipeg, Calgary, Edmonton, and Vancouver.

19. But we should not forget that we are a nation of diverse peoples and places.

20. Very diverse indeed.

Exercise 41-3 Correcting Fragments [II]

In the following exercise you are asked to correct any errors in sentence construction, whether they are run-on sentences or sentence fragments. A number of the sentences in the paragraph you are asked to edit are correct, so you need to be sure that a correction is called for. Please write the corrected paragraph in the lines provided for you.

It is startling to read that General Motors might disappear into bankruptcy before the end of 2009 this was, not long ago, the largest company in the world. What a shock. Among a host of reasons for the swift fall of GM are two central reasons. The first is the fact it has been unionized longer than any other car company, the second is their attachment to large vehicles The agreements that GM signed with unions as long as fifty years ago. The company Presidents and board members never foresaw that agreeing to pension plans would mean that the most expensive component in a Cadillac. It would be the $1,500 per auto coming out of a GM plant to pay for the medical and pension benefits of retired workers. Compare that amount to the $300 per auto Toyota pays. While also producing cars and trucks in the United States. But it was not only the failure of GM to prepare for the expenditures necessary to comply with the collective agreements it signed with its unions that placed it in jeopardy. While European and Asian manufacturers perfected compact vehicles powered by efficient four-cylinder motors. GM persisted in sending large number of vehicles to their showrooms that were built on a truck platform. Most frequently with a six- or eight-cylinder engine inside it. When times were good, consumers accepted the costs associated with gassing up and running such large vehicles, whether trucks or SUVs. But the combination of a brief but intense inflation of oil prices and a sudden deflation of the American economy. And other economies for that matter. GM was not ready for the collapse of its traditional market and the sudden decline of customers interested in large vehicles. Or in any vehicles at all. The Silverado truck was once a proud American icon. Having become a symbol of a manufacturer unable to perceive where the market was heading. Although the federal government has come to the aid of the three large American carmakers, their future remains uncertain, we do not know if there will be one, two, or three carmakers by the end of 2009. Or none.

Write a corrected version of this paragraph below.

Chapter 42 Agreement

Exercise 42-1 Subject–Verb Agreement

Find and correct the errors in subject-verb agreement in the following passage.

One of the financial analysts I read recently have dedicated his column to how the markets are manipulated. Neither the individual investor nor the large stockholders is aware of the forces that affect the value of their investments on a day-to-day basis. The large shareholders, as well as the small investor, is often unaware of the real reasons why investment prices fluctuate. Individual stocks or even the bond market rise and fall in ways that perplex analysts. The young investor and the old investor alike is told to hold on to an investment and to depend on its long-term appreciation. This and other sage advice is of little comfort when investors want access to the money tied up in their investment. An investment team that are studying the market to counsel its clients may have to reconsider its strategy. Every one of them want to retain his or her clients; without clients, investment counsellors would be out of work. Thus, some of the counsellors' advice are geared to maintaining the investment activity of clients. There is some counsellors, though, who may temper their advice, realizing that they have to protect their clients in the short term and wait for better returns and more commissions in the future. That, however, may not put food on their plates or money in their wallets in the short run. The problem of the counsellors are of little comfort to investors, who sees his investments below cost. How can investors feel comfortable knowing the market is manipulated in ways that they cannot foresee or fathom?

12 errors

Exercise 42-2 Verb Tense and Mood Agreement

In each of the following sentences you will encounter two possibilities. The first is that the sentence is correct. The second is that the sentence contains an agreement error, either an unnecessary shift in verb tense or an error in mood. If you need to refresh your memory on these matters, check mood and tense in Chapters 27 and 42.

For each sentence below, state either that the sentence is correct or that it has an agreement error. If it has an agreement error, state whether it is an error in tense or an error in mood. Write a correct version of the sentence in the space provided.

1. In 2007, Canadians are going south of their border to buy cars at reduced American prices.

   _____
   _____
   _____

2. One year later, they were not importing cars from the States; in fact, they were not buying as many Canadian cars either.

   _____
   _____
   _____

3. This change was a result of the collapsing economy. If GM was in charge of that economy, the cars would still be selling, and we would have more disposable income.

   _____
   _____
   _____

88   Part VIII   *Grammatical Sentences*

4. When the leaders of the American carmakers appeared in Washington before the Senate inquiry committee, they are foolish enough to be televised as stepping off private jets. Later, they wondered why senators criticized this choice of transportation.

___
___
___
___

5. One month later, when the same leaders appeared again to argue their need for government support, they are driving hybrids. Interestingly, at least one of those hybrids is an SUV, demonstrating they never fully understood the first criticism.

___
___
___
___

6. In the end, both the American and Canadian governments decide that support for the North American car industry is necessary. Many citizens in both countries felt the companies should be left to deal with their own mess.

___
___
___
___

7. If it was you making the decision, what would you do?

8. In some ways, a company like GM, which drives its stock value down from twenty-nine dollars a share in 2000 to two dollars and forty cents in 2008, deserved to be left to find its own way out.

9. But the politicians realize that there were an extremely large number of citizens who would be hurt by the failure of even one of the big three companies. For instance, the average salary of an auto assembly plant worker is nearly thirty-two dollars an hour.

10. Even a worker at a plant manufacturing auto parts averages twenty-four dollars an hour. If the auto maker was to fail and go into bankruptcy, tens of thousands of workers would turn overnight from citizens paying mortgages, taxes, and living expenses into unemployed people eligible for unemployment pay.

11. It was the sheer size of the automobile industry that intimidates elected representatives, driving them to vote money for support of the companies rather than following their instincts and leaving the private sector alone.

12. Not surprisingly, many elected representatives of right-wing parties followed their ideological values and refuse to vote support.

13. Again, if it had been you making this decision, what would you have done?

14. The great fear of all those who support the rescue of these companies must be the possibility that the rescue will not work in the end. Both GM and Chrysler desperately offered price reductions on their product and completed plans to lay off many more workers in light of the decreased demand in North America for new vehicles.

15. Ironically, if this reduction in demand was happening in 2010, GM would have the Volt, their new electric car, and a number of hybrids to offer the public's demand for autos offering low gas consumption.

Note: The facts used in this exercise were drawn from articles published in the *Vancouver Sun* on December 13 and 16, 2008. Those articles were David Akin, "Feds, Ontario offer 2 billion auto bailout," December 13, 2008: D4; Fiona Anderson, "Industry's global woes will be felt locally," December 13, 2008, D4; and Doron Levin and John Helyar, "Already bankrupt GM won't be rescued by U. S. loan," December 16, 2008: F5.

Exercises 42-3 Pronoun–Antecedent Agreement

In the following passage, find the errors in pronoun–antecedent agreement and correct them.

How many sets of wires connect your television, DVD, CD player, speakers, and tuner? For most folks, the area where all these items converge is spaghetti central. Ironically, the tangle of wires is just the overt symptom of the many small nagging puzzles that can arise when you connect a number of audio-video devices to one another. Even if you have only a DVD, a television, and speakers, you can be guaranteed it will give you problems. Add on a high-definition device like a PVR, a CD player, and a tuner, and suddenly complications arise. Neither the devices nor its wiring is simple or can be set up quickly. Each device has to be properly hooked up to the correct input sockets on the tuner for them to run correctly. Neither the CD player nor the DVD player will run on the same circuit as each has their own sound amplification needs. Even when you have successfully configured your system, operating malfunctions will still occur when you least expect it. One of the components loses their connections. Suddenly, there is no sound. You slide your components out to see what the problem is. Each of the wires has wrapped themselves around other wires, and you can't see clearly what connects to what. The wires all look the same. In addition, it is all tangled up with the other wires. It is not enough to find the one wire that appears to have a bad connection at one end; you have to trace them to the other end to make sure you have the right wire. Each wire and connection has to be checked to make sure they are secure.

10 errors

Exercise 42-4 Pronoun Reference Problems

Check the following sentences for errors in pronoun reference. Write "correct" in the space provided for any sentences that are correct. Correct each error in a sentence by rewriting the sentence in the space provided. If you are uncertain of the reasons behind faulty pronoun reference, reread Part VIII, Chapter 42, before doing this exercise.

1. Since anyone can attend the film showing tonight, it is hard to check them at the door.

   _____
   _____

2. Either the one-sided games or the increase in ticket prices are the reason for the decline in attendance at football games.

   _____
   _____

3. Some of the people arriving late are getting angry about how long it takes to enter the theatre.

   _____
   _____

4. Neither she nor her sisters is ready for the family holiday that starts next week.

   _____
   _____

5. The committee announced their recommendations after completing an investigation that occupied four months.

6. There is a number of reasons why you will not pass your statistics course this semester.

7. Each Christmas toy coming out of the Guangdong factory has had its paint checked for lead before being boxed for shipment.

8. The Canadian bomb disposal division will have their first scheduled break from duty next month.

9. Every person has to ensure that they have signed the proper forms before taking an approved holiday.

10. Many of the Americans who voted for a president in 2008 were casting their votes for the first time in their lives.

_____

_____

Exercise 42-5 Unclear Pronoun Reference

In the following paragraph, please check to ensure that none of the sentences have agreement errors or unclear reference problems. Once you have identified all the mistakes you can find, rewrite the paragraph in the space provided, eliminating all the mistakes.

One of the problems that are facing Asian food markets in 2009 is the shortfall in rice. Earthquakes, flooding, and interrupted growing seasons are a major part of the problem, but this has been compounded by wastage of what rice crops have been harvested. Spills, contamination by water, rats, and rot consume an estimated 15 percent of the harvested rice before it gets to the marketplace. Given that rice is a staple food throughout the region, these need to be addressed. The vermin and spillage problems interact because the holes eaten by vermin in sacks of rice let the rice fall out and decay on the floor. There is subsequent losses of product because of this simple problem. Many of the sacks holding the harvested rice have been crudely patched because of the cost of new sacks, and this contributes to the level of lost product. Another of the many reasons causing the harvested grain to decline before getting to market are the leaking of barn and warehouse roofs. Once water has soaked the rice, it is no longer edible. The rot is often a phenomenon of the methods used to dry the harvested rice. Laid out on roads and other flat areas to dry, rice often stays there too long. It may be run over by vehicles, corrupted by oil and other substances, eaten by birds, which decreases the size of the crop brought to market. The United Nations and individual countries have combined its forces to try and counter wastage. They know that the rice lost after harvesting and before marketing are sufficient to feed 184,000,000 people. A typical rice farm is small and its owner has

Chapter 42 *Agreement* **97**

little money. So buying poison to combat rats and mice, paying for new barn roofs, building special drying areas, and waterproofing trucks are beyond them as strategies to fight waste. Everybody has to do their part in addressing this, however, especially now that famine faces many of these areas.

Note: The facts in this paragraph have been drawn from Gale, Jason, and Luzi Ann Javier, "Rice wastage has become a world food shortage problem," *Vancouver Sun*, December 29, 2008, C3.

Chapter 43 Common Sentence Problems
Exercise 43-1 Misplaced Modifiers

Find the misplaced modifiers in the following passage and correct them by placing them next to the sentence element they modify.

Politicians have said in the past they would try and develop programs that are green, programs that will deal with the problem of global warming and the approaching shortage of petroleum products. Much of society's development stems from items that are derived from oil in a modern society. In *The Graduate,* one of the throwaway lines addressed to Dustin Hoffman, the main character of a popular 1960s movie, was that there was a great future in plastics. Indeed, you don't have to look very far to find out how plastics have almost become an integral element of our day-to-day lives. As I write this, my fingers are typing out the letters of each of the words on a plastic keyboard embedded in a plastic case. If you are holding a pen in your hand as you read this, it is likely almost made entirely of plastic. Ironically, when *The Graduate* was first released, most people laughed at the advice given to the new university graduate. We may not laugh so hard once we realize what our dependence on plastic means, especially as petroleum products that plastic are made out of are going to decline in the near future. Time will only tell if we adapt to rising oil prices and the effect that will have on so many products we are accustomed to using.

The effect of petroleum products on the environment, however, is manifest in many ways. If we went shopping, we most likely had our purchase packed thirty years ago in a paper bag. Suddenly, most of the packaging industry only shifted to producing plastic bags. Now, everywhere we go, we find our purchases placed in plastic bags unless we make a point of bringing along our own cloth bags. The number of plastic bags has developed into a major problem in garbage dumps. Not only do these plastic bags not biodegrade, but they also blow out of the garbage dump and into the nearby countryside. Sometimes, they get even into the water system and end up in the ocean where they play havoc with seabirds and fish.

10 errors

Exercise 43-2 Dangling Modifiers

The following passage contains dangling modifiers. Find them and correct them, using the space provided between the lines.

At the turn of the twenty-first century, the automobile industry in North America was looking at bigger and bigger cars, vans, and four-wheel-drive SUVs that were not economical or fuel-efficient. Looking back in time, cars had already been through one period in the early 1980s when the price of fuel increased rapidly and the car-buying public changed its priorities. The same change in consumer behaviour occurred in 2008, but whether or not manufacturers or car owners would heed the shift was uncertain. After almost a century of being seen as a symbol of success, car owners continued to take the advice of the auto industry and buy inefficient vehicles.

In 2008, something did happen that made people's heads turn. For the first time ever, the company that sold the most cars in the world was no longer a North American company. General Motors lost its mantle as the world's largest car manufacturer to Toyota, which outsold GM. Seeing fuel efficiency as something that affected their pocketbooks, efficient, well-built cars were more attractive to buyers than they had been before. Suddenly, the North American big three automakers were faced with a horrendous downturn in sales and unprecedented losses. Thinking of how to maintain their corporations, Washington and Ottawa were looked at as good sources of assistance. After all, the big three reasoned, as their CEOs got into their private jets, if we don't get aid, the number of people we will have to lay off will be politically unacceptable. Getting into their jets, the money already seemed a certainty. Thinking about the issue, the money could be justified. Caught up in their own delusion, the assembly line hummed as they had in the past. Ottawa. Yet as the auto industry was a mature industry, politicians reasoned that money should not be doled out without some strings attached, and they rejected the CEOs' proposals. Shamed and shunned, the CEOs of the big three returned to their corporations empty-handed. Discouraged by their reception, rethinking their strategy was as essential to their immediate survival as rethinking the line of automobiles they would roll off their assembly lines.

8 errors

Exercise 43-3 Misplaced and Dangling Modifiers

The following passage contains both misplaced and dangling modifiers. Find the modifier errors, identify them, and correct them using the space provided between the lines.

According to studies done recently, by 2024, peak oil production will occur. That means that, by 2024, the world will be producing the maximum oil flow it can expect from its known petroleum resources. Looking beyond that date, oil production will decrease, leaving the world with less oil and higher demand. If we think the past increase in the price of oil was an anomaly, we are mistaken. If demand continues to rise and oil consumption continues to increase, the world is headed for a major crisis. Going down the road we are on even five years without coming to terms with the technological shift that is urgently needed, oil will be in short supply and its price will start to spike again. This time, however, prices will not go down quickly. The world either has to come to terms with using less oil or find alternatives for it. The short period of time is coming to an end in which we have become accustomed to inexpensive oil and gas. Ironically, building exactly more roads for more cars may be the wrong thing to do at this juncture. Putting money into research on technologies that might help us cope with the dramatic shift that oil's shortage will necessitate might be a smarter alternative. Now building mass transit rather than encouraging more people to use their cars will help the situation, but building larger houses and more suburban communities, will not help.

Besides the problem of peak oil production being only a few years away, according to a January 17, 2009, article in the *Vancouver Sun,* "25 per cent of the world's reserves are overstated" (C2). If that is true, the peak production of oil may be closer than even experts think, and alternatives will be hard to implement soon enough to make a difference. Problems lie ahead in the immediate future. Given that we are worried about global warming, can we afford to switch our heating technology and electricity-generating technology back to coal? How will we cope with the rising cost of plastics and the many other by-products of petroleum? Similarly, the container, food storage, and general merchandise packaging manufacturers have components tied to oil. The shift away from oil or the increase in cost of oil-related goods will dramatically affect such industries. Finally, how do we rationalize the fact that, if post-industrial nations encourage energy conservation, the countries most affected will be emerging nations, where industrial growth and increased energy consumption are almost analogous to the growth of their whole economies?

Not paying close attention to this problem, a new Dark Age may be launched. It will be one caused not by cultural and religious intolerance but by a similar set of ignoble stances related to the consumption of energy. Whereas the Dark Age in Europe after the fall of the Roman Empire was figurative, the next Dark Age the world experiences may well be literal, as the lights and machines are switched off and we descend into a different type of human abyss. Looking ahead, how such a downturn in human activity will affect societies around the world remains to be seen. A profound downturn does suggest, though, that our current lifestyle will have to change. What all this means for political stability is anyone's guess.

4 dangling modifiers

6 misplaced modifiers

Exercise 43-4 Working with Parallel Structure

This exercise asks you to ensure that there are no faults with the handling of parallel structures in any of the following sentences. If you have difficulty with the exercise, please consult Chapter 43-d in Part VIII. For each of the sentences below, either write CORRECT in the space provided or a corrected version of the sentence.

1. One of the new phenomena in the lives of the affluent is the presence in their homes of nannies, whose responsibilities include cleaning the house, getting the children to school, cooking meals, and laundry as required.

   _____
   _____
   _____
   _____

2. In the United States, nannies sometimes become a political issue when elected people hire someone who does not possess a green card, a record of formal entry to America, fluency in American English.

   _____
   _____
   _____
   _____

3. Although it is not part of the nanny issue, Americans have expressed resentment about the number of illegal immigrants in their country, people working at jobs without holding green cards, voting without being formally registered, living in what amount to separate communities, and avoid military service.

4. I was struck by the brevity of the message posted by the apartment building's laundry room by the caretaker. It read: a) use your own soap; b) take dry clothes; c) don't leave your laundry alone; d) locking the door after use is required.

5. Most post-secondary institutions now have learning centres that attempt to help students to master the courses they are taking, write papers in those courses, to learn proper study techniques, and to learn how to prepare for time-limited tests.

6. The simple fact that about 30 percent of post-secondary students disappear between the first and third years of study suggests that either more care and funding need to be invested in these study centres or to change entrance requirements.

Chapter 43 *Common Sentence Problems*

7. Considering that, across Canada, the grade 12 cohort has shrunk in recent years, post-secondary institutions are spending more energy on recruitment than on student success; more money on residences than on counselling; more time searching for cheaper, less experienced faculty than on creating buddy systems or learning groups; and more time getting students to enroll with them than on ensuring those students are successful.

8. One of the major areas where students struggle is in completing papers on time. A student enrolled in a full load of courses in Humanities will probably be required to write ten or more papers in a fourteen-week semester, and that means starting research a month ahead of the paper's due date, draft a first effort early, and getting help from an instructor or a learning centre with that draft.

9. Most students don't fail because of ability. It is more likely that a drop-out is caused by a lack of motivation, parties on every weekend, an inability to plan a schedule that includes study and writing time, and a simple realization that it is too late to catch up once you have fallen behind.

_____
_____
_____
_____
_____
_____

10. Sadly, however, the disappearance of students after they have enrolled in a post-secondary institution robs Canada of educated workers, places youth at risk because of an inadequate preparation for the workplace, and puts too many people on unemployment paths.

_____
_____
_____
_____
_____

Chapter 43 *Common Sentence Problems*

Part IX USAGE AND DICTION

Chapter 44 Diction (Word Choice)

Exercise 44-1 Redundancy and Wordiness

Locate the redundancy and wordiness problems in the following passage and eliminate them by rewriting sentences.

When we learned the law of gravity that stated whatever goes up must come down, we did not understand that it also applied to other aspects of life beyond the laws of gravity that also go up and down. For instance, during the period between 1995 and 2007, everyone who was interested in investments thought that prices were going in one direction only, that they couldn't go anywhere but up. House prices climbed every year, and those who were new to the real estate market accepted realtors' assurances that today's prices were a bargain, for the people marketing the new developments were sure to boost the prices soon again as demand was higher than supply and when that happened the price would increase, it would keep going higher and higher. Listening to that assertion, some even thought that buying and flipping new condos was a good way to turn a fast profit; in a short period of time, they reasoned, they could earn a vast amount of money reselling their investment. For a down payment of five percent of the asking price, they could reap the reward of reselling the condo for a five percent increase in the selling price making for a big return on their small investment, a profit they could not obtain investing the same money in a savings account or other conservative investment. They did not factor in some of the other costs of such an investment—land transfer fees, real estate agent fees, or GST—which would eat into their profit margin. They had heard too many stories about people who had done well in real estate, people who had made more money in real estate than in any other kind of investment. There were even investment seminars some of them had attended that had promised them windfall profits through buying and flipping houses and condos, they too could make a fortune in a short period of time.

During this time, even real estate agents got caught up in the euphoria of buying and selling houses. These agents actively looked for older houses they could buy, cosmetically renovate with a quick paint job, and flip for a comfortable profit. This practice also had an inflationary effect on the market. Suddenly, the best bargains were only on the market for days. People competed with one another and outbid one another to get properties. Asking prices did not reflect the high selling prices that properties garnered; most houses were being sold above asking price and above the price that they had been assessed at for sale. It was being called a sellers' market and, suddenly, "fixer-uppers" or "handy man specials" did not last on the market. They sold as quickly, if not more quickly, than other, sounder houses. This also had a consequential effect on what was called entry level housing or housing for first-time buyers. Now, what had been affordable housing for first-time buyers, a new young couple starting off, was above their means in many urban markets in cities. Even though the government was telling everyone that inflation was running at a lower rate than it had in years, the housing market was spiralling out of control beyond the reach of many young Canadians. Suddenly, banks were offering thirty and thirty-five year mortgages, and people were looking at a future, where if they were to buy into the dream of owning their own house, they would have no disposable income, no money for holidays or the pleasures in life, for a very long time, until they retired.

Exercise 44-2 Correctness and Diction Levels

In the following exercise you are asked to pay special attention to the wording of the individual sentences of the paragraph. Wherever you find a word used incorrectly or used at an inappropriate level, make the necessary correction. If you need to refresh your understanding of levels, reread 44-c. For the purpose of this exercise, assume that the correct level for the diction is the formal level, which precludes using colloquial or excessively elevated diction. Please write out your corrected version in the space provided. There are 27 errors in diction in the following paragraph.

One of the unexpected effects of computers in our world is the extent to which they make us airheads. A recent experience in a Tim Hortons revealed one way this tendency manifests itself. I was there for the simplistic task of picking up bagels. When I ordered six bagels, the server hit some keys and asserted the price was $6.60. I have been effecting the same purchase for quite a while and therefore corrected her, pointing out that the real price was $3.49. She looked at me with that look that says, "Why do I get stuck with the yahoos?" and repeated the $6.60 price. I asked her if she would turn around and look at the listed prices and confirm the price for bulky bagels. Before very long, she had summoned a co-worker, who punched the same keys and said gimme $6.60. I repeated my suggestion about actually casting their eyeballs on the price list behind them. Eventually, a third worker arrived to clear up the contretemps. She explained to the other two how a single bagel's price was $1.10, but the special price for a bulk purchase of six to go was $3.49 and required a different sequence of keys. This whole aversion experience reminded me how our electronic chum is also an opponent in its tendency to oppress our common sense. We have all had the ha-ha experience of being

112 Part IX *Usage and Diction*

told by a server that we owe some over-the-top price for a purchase when we know that figure is wrong. But years of having a machine do the add-and-subtract bit for us have left us unable to apply our general sense of proportion to numbers. We should know that a burger and a pop can't cost $22.67, but the computer's omniscience befuddles us and we say whatever it tells us to say. This is, you know, not a big deal when all we're talking about is a price in a Tim Hortons outlet. But, in 2000, Enron duped tons of Americans (and Canucks too) so badly that we sent its stock price to $90.00 before the truth emerged about what they really had and they became worthless overnight. Their accounting buddies, the pros when it comes to numbers, were all part of the Arthur Anderson group and aided in the deception, So that company went belly up as a result, as they should have. But where was our common sense? Why didn't we ask them to fess up about their earnings to stock value ratio? More recently, where was our fiduciary common sense when we were investing heavily in sub-prime mortgages to people who couldn't qualify for a mortgage in a month of Sundays? That "we," of course, included pension funds, brainy bankers, and even our national pension plan sharpies. At this point you probably think I have extrapolated a little bitty point into a big deal, but the basic fact remains. We should have been applying our sense of numeric proportion and our basic knowledge about affordability, but we weren't. We get used to relying on some outside agent to make us savvy when we should be relying on our own basic sense.

Write your corrected version on the following pages.

Chapter 44 *Diction (Word Choice)*

Exercise 44-3 Clichés and Idioms

The following passage contains clichés and idiom errors. Locate the clichés and idiom problems and replace them with appropriate expressions.

Have you seen the television advertisements that ask what seems to be a sincere question: how can seniors turn the fixed equity they have built up in their homes into cash? We have been told that a man's home is his castle, but, suddenly, in conflict to everything we have been told, financial institutions are telling people who have managed to pay off their debt before retiring that it is now preferable going into debt again so that they can spend freely. Rather than having their lifestyle grind to a halt in retirement, they can have an awesome life in their golden years skipping through the tulips and having a ball. Old age and retirement, we are being told, is a time when good things come to those who wait. It is a time when people can believe firmly that they should not put off to tomorrow what they can do today.

Financial institutions are actually building upon people's belief that there is no place like home; they suggest that seniors are painting themselves into a corner when they don't need to. After all, with the equity they have in their homes, they have a bird in the hand, and they don't have to dream about the two in the bush. They are capable to use the money they have in their houses in accord to their wishes so that they can be independent to those around them. Most often, such programs are known as CHIPs or Canadian Home Income Plans, but they are also called reverse mortgages. In a reverse mortgage, a senior is told he or she can have a ball and not have to pay the piper. Reverse mortgage advertisements note that seniors do not have to pay any interest on the mortgage as long as they live in their house. They don't, however, tell the senior that,

116 Part IX *Usage and Diction*

even at prime mortgage rates, the interest on the mortgage will compound quickly. If a senior were to take out a CHIP for $100,000, an amount that looks a safe bet given that a large number of houses cost between $400,000 and $500,000 in Canada, the simple interest on that $100,000 after one year at even 5 percent, would total $5,000. In the second year, the interest would be calculated on $105,000 and be $5,250. Thus, the total amount to be repaid to the lending institution after just ten years would be $162,889.44 with an interest of $7,756.64 in the tenth year. If the senior were to live for twenty years, the interest accrued on the loan would total $165,329.68, and the loan would have a face value of $265,329.68. The question might be who is having their cake and eating it too, the senior or the bank? It is sad when financial institutions can take advantage of seniors in this manner. Seniors have to wake up and smell the coffee and complain about such deceptions.

21 errors

Chapter 45 Pronoun Case

Exercise 45-1 Pronoun Case

In the following sentences you will find a variety of errors in pronoun case. Some of the sentences are correct. Please make any corrections necessary so that no pronoun case errors remain. Refer to Chapter 45 if you are uncertain about any of your decisions.

1. The majority of Canadians, me included, believed that the economic growth of recent years would continue.

2. Our leaders had assured us that they would continue to have balanced budgets for the future and that they would use the surpluses to pay down historical debt.

3. Those of we who believed them are now aware that the leaders were wrong.

4. In early 2009, Stephen Harper, a staunch defender of balanced budgets, tabled a severely unbalanced budget, assuring us citizens that there was no alternative.

5. Clearly, the rapid decline of market values worldwide had caused him changing his position on deficit spending.

6. When other provincial politicians followed Harper's lead, we knew the conservative belief that governments should not impose their selves in the marketplace no longer applied.

7. Apparently, if governments in most industrial countries throw billions of dollars into public and private projects to stimulate a dead economy, it is hard for whomever commands a middle power like Canada to resist copying that lead.

8. Gordon Campbell of British Columbia followed the same path and it had been he who insisted that a deficit budget would never be tabled by any government he ran.

9. In many ways, Canada was simply following the lead of the American president, Barack Obama; it was he who first argued for the transfer of public monies to assist private business and fund economic activity.

10. No matter what we think of the abandonment of conservative values by conservative politicians, we can applaud the economic stimulus created by their choosing pragmatism over traditional policy.

Chapter 46 Pronoun Choice

Exercise 46-1 Pronoun Choice

Part A

In the following passage, you will find sentences where you have a choice between using the pronouns **who** *and* **whom,** *and* **which** *and* **that.** *Choose the pronoun appropriate for each sentence. If you are faced with choosing between* **which** *and* **that,** *you will also have to decide whether you need to place a comma before the pronoun you choose.*

Each spring in Canada, Canadians are bombarded with advertising by financial institutions **which/that/who/whom** advise us all to put money into tax savings plans called RRSPs and RESPs. It is a sure sign that tax season is upon us. **Who/Whom** can forget the campaign called "Freedom 55" **which/that** suggested if people put money away every year in an RRSP account, they would be able to retire at the young age of fifty-five rather than the traditional sixty-five ? Yet before you put money into one plan or the other, it is important to know **its/their** limitations and strengths. You have to know not only **who/whom** can put money into an RRSP or a RESP but also what advantages each of the plans holds for you.

The RRSP, the oldest of the two plans, is the one **which/that** most people have heard of. As a February 11, 2008, article by Sarah Dougherty in the *Montreal Gazette* titled "RRSPs Have Come a Long Way Since Introduction in the 1950s" notes, it was Louis St. Laurent's Liberal Party, just before it was defeated by John Diefenbaker's Conservatives, **who/whom/that/which** introduced RRSPs to Canada. At that time, there was no Canada Pension for retirees to depend on, and the government realized that

Canadians **who/whom** did not have access to a company pension could easily end up in poverty after they reached the then mandatory retirement age of sixty-five.

The question many Canadians ask in their youth is when should they start investing in an RRSP. Banks encourage people to place money in RRSP plans as the banks earn money from managing the funds. Interestingly enough, people forget that in many cases, management fees for RRSPs apply even in years when RRSPs lose money. Those **who/whom** put money into RRSPs would be wise to examine the management fees attached to the plan they are interested in to see whether the plan is a good investment for them. Some plans **which/that** advertise their returns do so in ways **which/that** can be deceiving to those **who/whom** are interested in them. As well, those interested in saving money might think about possible alternatives. Placing money in a retirement savings plan **which/that** will give them money upon retirement may not be a priority if they have other, more pressing financial needs. People have to think about **who/whom** they are giving the money to and whether they have a pressing need **which/that** should be met now. After all, students paying taxes at the rate of 18 percent should realize that all they are going to defer is the tax on the money they place in an RRSP. There is a likelihood that their marginal tax rate, if they end up getting a good job after they have finished their education, will eventually put them in a tax bracket that is higher than 18 percent when they retire. There is more than one way of looking at RRSP plans; that is something **whoever/whomever** considers them should know.

16 errors

Part B

Locate and correct the problems in pronoun choice in the following continuation of the above passage.

In good times, RRSPs may be the vehicle of choice for those that wish to save for their retirement, but with a host of products out there, many of which look like one another, the question most people have is "Which should I choose?" Questions like this are not simple to answer. An examination of the many plans which are in the marketplace could be time consuming. As well, an RRSP product that has performed well in the past may not perform well in the future. Investors whom have examined the different plans know that comparing one RRSP option with another is like comparing apples and oranges. Anyone that is investing in an RRSP should consider both the mix of assets in a plan and the plan's Management Expense Ratio or MER. It is not worthwhile to invest in a secure RRSP plan which will bring you an extremely low return when that plan's return all but disappears once the MER is applied. In a case like this, whatever you do in an RRSP might be worse for you than what you could do outside of an RRSP. Whoever said choosing a good RRSP was simple?

5 errors

Chapter 48 Inclusive Language

Exercise 48-1 Inclusive Language

In the following passage, identify the problems in inclusive language and substitute words that are inclusive.

You are saving a down payment for the purchase of your own condo, your own castle? You remember that every man looks forward to being the master of his domain, a king in his own realm. Everyone looks to a future when he can gaze out on his backyard complete with BBQ, deck, and gardens and enjoy the privacy that the fruits of his labour have given him. Yes indeed, there is no place like home. Young couples look forward to having a place of their own, complete with a two-car garage, a big-screen television, pets and a child or two. Even though our cousins to the south might think we live in igloos like Eskimos, in general, housing in Canada is very similar to housing in the U.S. Yes, mankind has come a long way from the days when a handy cave made a good home.

Yet the modern Canadian family unit is living in a more complex community than it did in the past and thinks of housing differently than previous generations. Urbanites in Canada, in fact, live in a complex, blended culture. Instead of looking forward to owning a suburban rancher, having two children, and being surrounded by people from the same ethnic background, modern urban Canadians who are purchasing their own residence are more likely to live in a condo close to the urban core and be surrounded by a variety of peoples and a variety of neighbours, including homosexual couples and families from a wide range of ethnic backgrounds, such as those from the Indo-Canadian, Oriental, and Afro-Canadian communities. In fact, when a community organization forms, it is not unlikely that the chairman of the organization has to recognize the complex elements in the organization and the complex nature of his urban neighbourhood. When organizing community events, the chairman has to be wary of old wives' tales and be careful to man and run programs with care to ensure that their programs are not exclusionary to people who have different sexual preferences.

21 errors

Chapter 50 Active and Passive Voice

Exercise 50-1 Active and Passive Voice

The following exercise asks you to convert passive voice to active voice. Each sentence is cast in passive voice; in the space provided below each sentence, rewrite the sentence in active voice. If necessary, consult Chapter 50 before doing the exercise.

1. Recently, the world was alerted to a remarkable scam that affected a large number of people.

2. The most notable element in the scheme that slowly came into public view was the total amount of money lost by the investors, 65 billion dollars.

3. The fraud was identified as a "Ponzi scheme," a business deal where the money taken from one investor is used to make a payment to a previous investor.

4. Another name that has been used to describe this particular swindle is a pyramid scheme, a deception that can be successful as long as new investors keep investing.

5. As the story was told in the newspapers, the special nature of the fraud was the fact that an unusual number of high-profile investors were involved and that the total monies lost was the largest ever recorded in such a scheme.

6. High-profile New Yorkers, a major New York charity, well-known Hollywood people, and even the retired manager of a hedge fund were found among the thousands of defrauded investors.

7. At least one suicide was the result of the loss of money caused by the deception, an investor who had put over a billion dollars into this fake investment.

Chapter 50 *Active and Passive Voice*

8. The perpetrator of this pyramid scheme was identified as Bernard Madoff, a New Yorker who had been a well-respected figure in the New York social world.

9. How such a simple fraud could have been maintained for so long and have involved so many supposedly sophisticated investors is one of the mysteries of the whole affair.

10. Ironically, it has now become clear that the scheme would still be going on if it hadn't been exposed because many investors attempted to recover their monies to cover other investments that collapsed because of the general implosion of the American economy at the end of 2008.

Part X PUNCTUATION

Chapter 52 The Comma

Exercise 52-1 The Comma

Add or take out commas in the following passage according to the rules for comma use in your text.

Part A

An article in *Maclean's* titled "This Computer Is So Me"[1] sums up the problems of the age only too well: mass manufacturers have realized that people prize their individuality. They don't want to dress the same as everyone else buy the same food or think the same thoughts. As such corporations are trying to stress that their products whether they be hamburgers, computers or automobiles can be customized to suit every individual's taste. It seems, we've come a long way from Henry Ford's comment about the Model T Ford: "You can have it any color you like, as long as it's black." Ford was interested in producing automobiles that everyone could afford. He believed people would accept mass-produced products. Currently people seem to be rebelling against the fact that manufacturers can produce goods cheaply as long as they have large production runs and an efficient production line. The irony lies in the fact that people still want to pay mass-production prices for goods that appear to be custom made. That is the secret to contemporary marketing and advertising. Today as the *Maclean's* article notes, corporations want you to think you are making decisions that personalize what you are buying. All the way from the lowly hamburger to the expensive automobile, corporations are giving you choices that make it seem like you are in control you are making the decisions. The slogans that they are using to reinforce this are emblematic of that sensibility. "Choose to have it your way" Burger King's slogan is even prominently displayed on the corporation website at the top of the nutrition page. However the use of you or in this case me is not new to the advertising world. Macdonald's use of slogans that put you the individual consumer in the centre of their advertisements started in 1967 when they used the slogan "McDonald's is Your Kind of Place" and followed that up with the 1971 slogan the one people remember even today "You Deserve a Break Today."

19 errors

Part B

The issue of targeting people's desire to be individual is not limited to inexpensive items like fast food. It goes far beyond that. As Lianne George points out in her article adapted from the book she wrote with Steve Maich *The Ego Boom: Why the World Really Does Revolve Around You* corporations like Dell Computers have taken the concept and applied it to the purchase of computers online. Dell which is famous for its online computer sales saw the retail market becoming flat but the company quickly noticed that what people wanted was choice; they did not all want the same things in their computer. Rather than giving people a standard computer that would include items most users wanted Dell decided to build sales and computers using an online decision tree. At the bottom of the tree customers are faced with basic choices including the size of the hard drive the size of the RAM the types of drives and the type of chip used to run the computer. After that the choices include what type of software the buyer wants, the type of monitor the size of the monitor and the screen's definition. As prospective customers add items they want to their "custom built computer" they can see how each item affects the total price. Buying a computer with Dell's online site, as opposed to going into a store and searching out the one that is right for you suddenly, becomes a totally different experience. Not only can prospective customers tailor their computer to their needs but, once they have finished "assembling" their personal computer they will then receive step-by-step e-mails telling them that their computer is being ordered assembled packed and finally shipped to them. Although Dell has copied the concept of personalizing that has been utilized by others, it has done so in a unique way that makes the decision tree on its website one that reinforces the idea that consumers are "customizing" their purchase to their needs. Henry Ford couldn't have done it better. Dell figured out how to get consumers utilizing the decision tree to get the assembly line to produce exactly what they want. Nothing is wasted; Dell does not even need retail outlets to produce sales.

1. Lianne George. "This Computer is so Me," *Maclean's*, February 2, 2009, pp. 52–55.

25 errors

Chapters 53 and 54 The Semicolon and the Colon

Exercise 53/54-1 The Semicolon and the Colon

In the following exercise you are asked to decide where a semicolon or a colon should be placed in the sentence to make its punctuation correct. Please use the space provided below each sentence to write in your choices. Simply put the word preceding the semicolon or colon you are adding to indicate its position.

1. It is impossible to read the daily news and not be struck by the irony implicit in many reports frequently, we see that our attempts to control events fail.

   _____

2. The reason for the irony is always the same our planning doesn't take in enough factors.

   _____

3. A recent example from the *Vancouver Sun* illustrates this phenomenon in this instance, good planning failed to anticipate what the future might bring.

   _____

4. Vancouver enjoys a significant business in unloading shipping containers for several reasons it is the largest western port in Canada, it is relatively close to large Asian economies, and it has access to the major cross-Canada highway.

   _____

5. Consequently, Vancouver and Prince Rupert have both expanded their port facilities behind this assumption was the expectation that West Coast ports would continue to enjoy expanding container business.

   _____

6. However, this assumption did not factor in three developments the Panama Canal is being significantly widened, global warming is increasing the likelihood that our Northwest Passage will be open water in the summertime, and transportation by water is the cheapest means of moving containers of goods.

    _____

7. There is also another factor at play here the largest density of people in North America live in the east of Canada and the United States.

    _____

8. This means the largest markets and industrial zones are also in the east typically, therefore, this is the main destination for containers and the products they hold.

    _____

9. Given the fact that transportation by water is much less expensive than transportation by road, Asian business may soon have several options they can, if they wish, ship containers directly to eastern North American markets using the widened Panama Canal they may even be able to use the Northwest Passage, open most of last summer, to reach our eastern cities, or they can renegotiate the fees currently in effect by threatening not to use our port any more.

    _____

10. Naturally, we did not anticipate these developments when we committed to expansion of our container capacity equally, we couldn't predict that a worldwide recession would diminish the number of containers being shipped from countries like China to Canada's West Coast.

    _____

11. This is, therefore, the basis of the irony with the best of intentions and careful planning, we commit to a plan of action that turns out to be questionable.

   _____

12. As the *Sun* column pointed out, American ports like Long Beach/Los Angeles have already experienced a decline in traffic it is distinctly possible that our expanded port facilities will end up serving fewer customers rather than more.

   _____

This exercise used data and thoughts from the following source:

Pete McMartin, "Vancouver Port May Be Left Waiting for Its Ships to Come In," *Vancouver Sun,* February 17, 2009, A1.

Chapter 55 Quotation Marks

Exercise 55-1 Quotation Marks

In the following sentences, you will find errors in the use of (or failure to use) quotation marks. In the space provided below each sentence, write any necessary corrections. If the sentence is correctly punctuated, write "correct."

1. "Can you believe how picky the officials were at the halfpipe competition?", asked most of the competitors at the snowboard test event hosted by Cypress Mountain, near Vancouver.

2. Cypress Mountain officials defended their cancellation of the parallel giant slalom by stating: "We feared there was not enough time to get the area designated for the event ready in accordance with international specifications. Additionally, we have to serve our own members, and it was our view that they would not have appreciated losing another afternoon on what they regard as their hill. You have to remember that this is just a test event to see how the area can be set up for an Olympic event."

3. I did hear one person attending the event observe, "Why does a great event like this have to be brought down by officialdom?"

4. One of the headlines on the blog of a person who attended reinforced this view read, "great scenery, picky people in charge."

5. On the CTV show *Sunday Sports Highlights*, the cameras emphasized the spectacular surroundings pleasing all who attended this event.

6. It is equally interesting to hear the number of critical comments made by traditionalists who lament the decision to include halfpipe and snowboardcross events in the Winter Olympics, feeling this decision represents a foolish Xification of the Olympic competition.

7. One element that received no criticism was the judges' decision in the halfpipe competition that gave Shaun White first place. In the words of one impressed fellow competitor, Shaun's run was seriously sick.

8. Many observers also stressed, after looking more closely at the hundreds of fans watching the competition: "where are all the forty and fifty year olds"?

9. Certainly, the crowds were predominantly people in their teens and twenties, dressed in clothes reminiscent of the dress of the competitors, talking in a special language about the halfpipe being under vert, an expression apparently referring to the vertical lips of the halfpipe run.

10. Overall, the event was a qualified success; in the words of one snowboarder it was a happening, and it showed the world we have arrived, so get used to us.

Chapter 56 The Apostrophe

Exercise 56-1 The Apostrophe

Find the errors in apostrophe use and correct them.

It started off simply enough. It wasnt even something that people paid much attention to. After all, the apostrophe is such an insignificant punctuation mark. Who wouldve thought that it would come to the point where a city in Britain, Birmingham, decided to officially drop the apostrophe from all its road signs. A friend of ours, Maureen, sent us an article in the *Globe and Mail,* "Trust the British to Make Apostrophes a Class Issue," that comments on Birminghams decision and notes one of the reasons why Birmingham think's the apostrophe should be dropped from street names is GPS units that cant locate streets on a map if there is an apostrophe in the name. In Birminghams case, "St. Paul's Square," for instance, is being changed to "St. Pauls Square" so that the GPS units can recognize the location. One of the Birmingham counsellor's observes that, as the street names in question are no longer owned by anyone, there is no need to use the apostrophe, but, more to the point, he argued that apostrophes "confuse people. If I want to go to a restaurant, I don't want to have an A-level in English to find it."

When Nav Sangha, a former student of mine, sent me a copy of Lynne Truss book *Eats Shoots and Leaves,*[1] I was fascinated. Truss points to the fact that, in Britain, the apostrophe has been abused for a long time, and it isnt just the possessive apostrophe that is not being used properly. She gives examples like "Ladie's hairdresser," and "Freds' restaurant" to illustrate the kinds of mistakes people are making with possession (52). She notes that people are confused about when to use "whose" and "who's" as well (61). Whose right, you might ask? We ought to know; it isnt that difficult.

Common in both Britain and Canada are misuse problems in business advertising and signs. Next time you pass a McDonalds, look at the restaurants sign. Then look at a Tim Hortons sign. When you do, you will know who uses the possessive form correctly. You will also know how, using the two corporations spelling, to correct these two names to assign possession correctly for this exercise. Then you can go online to Google and check for the correct spelling of the Hudsons Bay Company and the store Timothy Eaton started, Eaton's. More recent corporations tend to be at fault more often. For instance, the western Canadian restaurant Earls leaves out the apostrophe. It is no wonder that people are confused. Its all around us, signs that don't follow the rules for possession and the use of the apostrophe!

1. Lynne Truss, *Eats Shoots and Leaves* (New York: Gotham-Penguin, 2004).

17 errors

Chapters 57, 58, and 60 The Slash, Parentheses, and the Dash

Exercise 57/58/60-1 The Slash, the Dash, and Parentheses

In the following exercise you are asked to identify the places in sentences where the punctuation is incorrect. Please insert the correct punctuation, whether it is a slash, a dash, or parentheses. You can write your correction in the space provided below each sentence by writing the correct punctuation and the words that precede and follow it.

1. Watching the X-games on television reminds me that these games conceived in the last five years and passionately adopted by a special subculture are specifically designed to appeal to a young audience.

   _____

2. The *Winter Games* version is offered in both night and day versions the latter possible only through strong lighting and physically limited venues that allow the television channels to appeal to both a daytime and a nighttime audience.

   _____

3. One of the signs that the audience for this invented sport is young is the unique designs of the boardsharnesses used for the different competitions.

   _____

4. They are designed for short, stubby "skis" that have the capacity to turn sharply, glide easily, hold the boots to the "skis" during jumps and flips, and perhaps the key element work within more tightly-defined spaces than regular skis can do.

   _____

5. During the 2008 2009 season of the Winter X games, I watched several competitions and noted the distinctive dimensions of this new winter sport.

6. The competitors average age twenty-three virtually all had nicknames that reflected their status in what amounted to a counterculture and hair styles that echoed that culture and their youth.

7. The two forms of competition I watched, the snowboardcross and halfpipe, both echoed and as I saw it contrasted with the regular competitions they were derived from.

8. The halfpipe consisted of a U-shaped run cut in the snow that allowed the competitors to perform complex air manoeuvres in the tradition of gymnastics, while probably the intention limiting the run to a completion of the downhill length of that U-shaped run.

9. The competitors in this run must move strictly from side to side of the run, launching themselves into the air through the aid of the sharply vertical sides to the wonder and applause of the watching crowd and constantly advancing down the length of the run.

10. The snowboardcross competition features the contestants in helmets and different-coloured bibs racing over small hills and around curves over what appeared to be a half-mile course to see who could come first or third actually in the heats and advance to the final.

Punctuation Review

Exercise 52/60-2 Punctuation Review

In the following exercise you will find errors in the comma, semicolon, colon, question mark, hyphen, dash, and apostrophe. Cross out, replace, or add punctuation where necessary.

There is one famous quotation that everyone who has watched the old movie *Field of Dreams* remembers. This catchy little quotation becomes emblematic of the core theme of the movie a theme that actually reflects human behaviour over the past twenty years as we build bigger more complex communities. It seems innocuous at first and slightly silly when Kevin Costners character Ray Kinsella, hears a voice that intones a vague comment "If you build it, he will come." He does not completely understand this comment a comment he eventually links to building a baseball field on his farm. Yet this comment sets the tone for the strongest set of fantasies about land development and ownership of the past twenty years. I hadnt realized how this film related to the trends of the past twenty years until just recently but we all know that development drives population movement. Remember the last scene of the film. After the baseball field has been built, and the main character has played catch with his long dead father the camera pans back and shows a long line of car lights heading up the road to the Kinsella farm in the middle of Iowa. From this image we are supposed to infer that the farms future has been secured the dream has been realized and the family will live happily ever after. Something eerily similar has happened to our society, over the past twenty years people have bought into the dream that, if they buy property the prices will keep going up, if they want better roads for their commute into the urban centre or out to the suburbs bigger wider roads and bridges will be built to accommodate the increased volume of traffic. No one has stopped to think about what all this does to the land the city occupies to land utilization or to urban sprawl which generates many energy inefficiencies. Instead everyone simply wants one thing to "live happily ever after."

Maybe it is time we started to look at urban development and our expectations through a different lens, maybe we need to rethink our lifestyles our way of living, and use a different set of values when planning our communities and, our residences. You only have to ask yourself one question to prove that this is so what happens if we do nothing and continue building our urban communities and their surrounding suburbs the way we have over the past two decades.

To understand what is happening, all one has to do is look at the density of Canadas urban centres and compare the density of these cities to other urban centres in the world. According to the website citymayors.com Canada's largest city Toronto had in January 2007 a population density of 2,650 people per square kilometre and a total population of 4,367,000. At this time it was the 97th most densely populated city in the world. The most densely populated city which had 29,650 people per square kilometre and a total population of 14,350,000 people was Mumbai, India. Madrid Spain which had a slightly bigger population than Toronto with 4,900,000 people had a population density of 5,200 people per square kilometre and was the 42nd most densely populated city in the world. Vancouver, Canadas third largest city for all its boasts about being strongly connected to the environment and environmentalism had a population density of 1,650 people per square kilometre with a total population of 1,830,000 people and was 123rd in the list for urban density.

How we deal with urban density will not only decide whether our cities are sustainable but whether they will suffer from urban blight and degradation of the surrounding hinterland. The development of cities has too often been subject to the whims of developers who have short term gains in mind not long term goals. They are not interested in the future of the cities they help develop, they are interested in the future of their bottom line. Sadly quite a number of cities have councils dominated by individuals who have ties to realtors and developers and this has meant that town planning has not always been governed by sustainable principles instead planning has been governed by greed. Because of this problem the future of our largest urban centres and their densities is not being governed by principles that augur well for the future. Would an investigation of whether cities follow the principles of good governance be in order. Would it be a good idea for cities to consider the relationship between development, density, and future problems. Should cities be judged on how they deal with urban blight urban poverty. The bottom line is, cities have to think about the future now. What roads transportation systems housing density and industry cities put in place today will define the infrastructure and urban problems of the future.

1. All of the specific statistics on cities taken from http://www.citymayors.com/statistics/largest-cities-density-125.html

Part XI MECHANICS

Chapter 63 Capitalization

Exercise 63-1 Capitalization

The following exercise asks you to examine each sentence and determine whether the rules of capitalization have been followed correctly. If they have been, write "Correct" in the space provided beneath the sentence. If not, identify the error or errors in the sentence in that space.

1. When the Olympics are opened to the world in February 2010, we can expect Stephen Harper, our Prime Minister, and Premier Gordon Campbell of B.C. to be prominent in the official ceremonies.

   _____
   _____

2. The opening ceremonies are scheduled for BC place, the stadium built more than twenty years ago and scheduled to be refurbished following the Olympic games of 2010.

   _____
   _____

3. One of the most interesting venues for these games will be the Richmond olympic oval, the building designed to house the long-track speed-skating competitions.

   _____
   _____

4. This building was opened in 2009 by Mayor Malcolm Brodie, one of the more prominent Mayors in metropolitan Vancouver.

5. "While the short-term function of this building will be to house Olympic events," announced Brodie at the opening, "We know that it will eventually be a major community centre for many activities."

6. The Oval is a spectacular building visually and a provocative building politically.

7. It first gained political fame because the originally estimated cost of $50 to 60 million became $180 million upon completion; Richmond's city council took heat for the escalation of costs.

8. Additionally, it was built on a flood plain; this caused problems for a building required to meet rigorous Specifications dictated by the Olympic speed-skating council.

9. One of its unique features is the arched roof whose interior is finished with wood reclaimed from trees killed by the Pine Beetle infestation that attacked B.C. forests some years ago.

10. This enormous roof has attracted international attention and was a source of great pride for Vanoc, the Vancouver Olympic committee charged with responsibility for all the olympic facilities.

11. Unfortunately, while a brilliant visual effect, the roof was found to have water penetration problems, and the dispute is ongoing about whether the repairs should be paid for by Richmond city council, Vanoc, the roofing construction association of B.C., or the builder.

12. Not surprisingly, other Municipalities in B.C.'s Lower Mainland are secretly happy they are not involved; they are interested is seeing how it will all turn out.

13. In the meantime, B.C.'s liberal and New Democratic parties are keeping as far away from the dispute as they can, and the provincial legislature has had no comment.

_____

_____

14. The Richmond public has spoken, however; they turned out in large numbers to the opening, skated on the Oval track as soon as they could, and made it clear to the Richmond city council that all Richmond citizens should be proud of this striking Olympic and City facility.

_____

_____

_____

15. Perhaps most important, the international Olympic Committee gave their unanimous approval of the oval when they toured it in the spring of 2009.

_____

_____

Chapter 64 Abbreviations

Exercise 64-1 Abbreviations

In the following exercise, choose the correct abbreviation for each situation.

1. Aba./Alta. is the abbreviation for the province that has, as its two main cities, Edmonton and Calgary.

2. Prof. Higgins/Professor Higgins is the name of the central male character in *My Fair Lady*.

3. Gov. Gen./Governor General Michaëlle Jean was born in Haiti, and French is her first language.

4. When you write a letter in Canada and you are sending it to Newfoundland, you must make sure you use the proper Canada Post abbreviation, which is Nfld. and Lab./NL.

5. There is a strong history of documentary film production in Canada, and historically, most of those films were made by the National Film Board of Canada, which is most often referred to as the NFBC/NFB.

6. If there is a strike in Ottawa, the government most often speaks with the leaders of the Canadian Union of Public Employees or CUOPW/CUPE, a union representing about a half-million workers.

7. Though in the past, the most common practice in Canada was to designate dates using the Christian era signifiers a.d./AD and bc/BC, today the more acceptable era designations are BCE/B.C.E. and CE/C.E., which stand for Before the Common Era and Common Era respectively.

8. When introduced as Dr. Marvin Gold Ph.D., Dr. Gold always felt as if his credentials were overwhelming his personal identity.

9. Now that most popular style manuals no longer use Latinate terms, it is very rare that you see such terms as loc. cit./Loc. Cit., which is the abbreviation for the Latin *loco citato* and means "in the place cited."

10. Federal political parties in Canada may carry the same names or similar names as provincial parties. If ever you were unsure of whether they stood for the same policies federally and provincially, you had only to look at the political views of the federal ndp/NDP and some of the provincial parties by the same name. How much in common the bq/BQ in Ottawa has with the pq/PQ in Quebec might be another interesting question. Similarly, the Liberal party and the Conservatives certainly have different agendas provincially and federally.

Chapter 65 Numbers

Exercise 65-1 Numbers

In the exercise below, you are asked to correct any errors in the correct use of numbers in written work. The sentences of the paragraph are numbered so that you can identify the error by sentence number and write in the correction in the place provided beside the sentence number. If you are uncertain which style to follow, the exercise is intended to follow the MLA rules about using numbers in written work.

(1) Recently, we have been introduced to large numbers being used in newspapers, news reports, and even conversation. (2) We are told, for instance, that the Iraq War has now cost the United States over one trillion dollars. (3) Yet if you go to another source, the assumed amount becomes two 000, 000, 000, 000 dollars. (4) And a source that includes money paid to all private and semiprivate contractors estimates that three trillion dollars is the most accurate figure. (5) The problem is, of course, that most of us have very little idea of how much money a trillion dollars is. (6) So let's consider some simpler examples. (7) Mats Sundin, the hockey player, earns an annual salary of $10,000,000. (8) He would have to work for one hundred thousand years to reach the magic one trillion mark. (9) Maybe you want a comparison that is closer to home. (10) As a professional executive, you might expect an annual salary of eighty thousand dollars. (11) In that case, you could hope to amass 1 trillion dollars by the year twelve million five hundred two thousand ten on January 1, if that is the anniversary date of your hiring. (12) We are therefore talking about a seriously large figure. (13) If you invested that trillion dollars at a 4% rate of return annually, you

would find yourself earning three billion three hundred thirty-three million three hundred thirty-three thousand three hundred thirty-three dollars and thirty-three cents every month of the year. (14) You could probably take a good holiday for that kind of money. (15) Perhaps a fairer estimate is to ask how much each citizen of the United States owes to pay off the three trillion dollars expended in Iraq. (16) That brings us a much more comprehensible number of thirty-three hundred thirty-three dollars and thirty-three cents. (17) Nevertheless, we need to be careful when politicians start talking about trillions or, in Canadian terms, 1,000,000,000s of dollars. (18) We blithely repeat the word "trillion," but we have little real sense of what the number means.

Use the following to record your corrections. If a sentence has no errors, write "correct" in the space provided.

1. _____
2. _____
3. _____
4. _____
5. _____
6. _____
7. _____
8. _____
9. _____
10. _____
11. _____

12. _____

13. _____

14. _____

15. _____

16. _____

17. _____

18. _____

Chapter 66 Hyphens

Exercise 66-1 Hyphens

Where necessary, add or take out hyphens in the following exercise.

Part A

I have decided we are living in a very strange, out of touch world. Students in British Columbia are paying more in tuition fees per year than corporations in the province are paying in taxes. It seems we have, as a society, decided that it is more important to support the bottom line of businesses than to support the future of our country or first class education for the next generation of Canadians. In effect, we are supporting an implicit class system whereby the wealthy can afford to have their offspring educated in the best state of the art jobs. In contrast, the poor and the middle class will have to go into debt or have their children go into debt to manage to get a decent education and a quasi decent job. How sad is this? On top of this, we have people now supporting negative population growth wherein a whole generation will not produce offspring. Someone needs to rethink the consequences of these ideals for the next generation. We are creating a society that is anti family, anti education, and anti democratic. Is it old fashioned to think about the family unit and its future? We are creating a society where the few will have much, the many will have next-to-nothing, and the people who have reached the not so golden years after retirement will not be supported by government programs as the country will be missing a whole generation of young people and, therefore a whole generation of people who are working and paying taxes. Have we suddenly forgotten what a social contract is? Do we no longer believe in family or extended family groupings? How fragmented and dys-functional are we prepared to let our society become in the name of support for corporate bottom lines and fuzzy notions about sustainability?

11 errors

Part B

A quick look at the cost of a postsecondary education is very informative. We think it is important for young adults to have skills that are up-to-date. Even knowing how to use a word processing program and how to use e-mail to send and receive documents are essential skills that students must have at the beginning of their studies. If they don't have computer and on-line skills, they may find themselves disadvantaged when it comes to course selection or course availability. Out of thirty five courses a student may want to take, he or she may find that as many as ten may only be offered on-line. This fact may put a course out of reach for a student who does not have the requisite computer skills. It may sound self evident, but access at home to a computer, just like access to a supportive family, may make or break a student's performance. We may think it unCanadian that people be discriminated against because of their socio economic background, but it is a fact of life today in Canada, in the same way that where people live may affect their ability to get a good education and a good job.

7 errors

Answer Key

Part I THE WRITING PROCESS

Chapter 2 Prewriting II: Techniques

Exercise 2-1 Applying the Pentad

All of the exercises for Chapter 2, "Prewriting II: Techniques," are distinctive in that there is no single "correct" response. The intention of the exercises is to give you an opportunity to work with techniques that will help you discover and organize ideas and materials for any essay you are assigned in any course. The discussions that follow about each of the Chapter 2 exercises should therefore be seen as illustrative rather than prescriptive. In your responses, you may well have taken a different direction from the ones that follow. We have provided sample answers simply to give you answers to compare to your own.

ACT

This should be one of the Pentad's terms where there is little likelihood of disagreement. The "Act" is the *Idol* series, the Fox program that so quickly became a program with a high viewer response. You may well have added details that you think are key to the series' appeal to the North American and other audiences that responded so favourably. Those details could begin with the particular sequence that FremantleMedia adopted for the series. That sequence includes the first stage, the auditioning, the second stage, the semifinals, and the last two stages: the final and grand finale. This sequence aims to increase the audience's interest as favourite competitors are adopted by viewers and then either succeed or drop away. Another key element is the voting dimension of the "Act." The voting, by electronic submission, gives viewers a stake in the results as well as a feeling of participation. It also provides a corrective to the professional judgments of the panel of judges. Additionally, the voting allows regional favouritism an outlet and allows a normally passive audience to be active.

AGENT

Here is the area where we expect the greatest divergence from our suggested answer to appear in your response. There are three possible choices you might develop as well as an optional fourth, depending how extensive your analysis was of this Pentad element.

The first and perhaps most obvious choice would be the producer and the presenter of the series, FremantleMedia and Fox Television. In the simplest sense, there would be no *Idol* series if it hadn't been produced and exhibited. This suggests one answer. If you choose this duo, your responses regarding

"Agency" and "Purpose" will follow from this choice. Also, if this is your choice, you may well have added details about FremantleMedia and Fox.

A second choice here would be the contestants. There would be no *Idol* series if there were no contestants. From the early stages, when more applicants are discarded than approved, to the last stage, when a single contestant becomes the Idol of the Year, the audience is attracted and held by the contestants, who seem to be the focus of the series. Thus it is easy to defend a position that defines the performers as the natural "Agents" of the series.

A third "Agent"—the audience—is equally defensible. We all realize that no television program or series can last eight years if there is no audience. The size of the audience dictates the size of the profit available to the television company—that is why there are "free" programs on television. In this case there is an additional factor: the audience has a direct influence on the success of the contestants and in one sense determines who the new Idol will be. This endows the audience with additional weight, and that may have led you to define the television audience as the "Agent."

Though it is unlikely that you chose a fourth option, there is a possible alternative. If you believe that the audience's fanatical attachment to a favourite contestant is the key element of the series, you may have identified the "American Dream" as the "Agent." American culture is unique in that it embraces the dream that America is the one place in the world where a person can rise from anonymity to fame and success. If you believe that the most powerful influence on the audience is their wish to see an unknown contestant become famous and wealthy in the course of four-and-a-half months, you can make a case for the American Dream as the most powerful agent behind the success of the *Idol* series. Even the word "Idol" seems instructive in this context.

AGENCY

Given the nature of the preceding discussion, you may predict that the "Agency" part of the Pentad leads to elements already touched on. Obviously, the simplest part of the "Agency" is the medium that brings the series to the audience. That includes the producer, the television company and channel, the advertisers, and the whole profit motive underlying the presentation of the series. The more complex part of the "Agency" here is the cultural prism that underlies the broadcasting of the series and the audience's reception of, and response to, that series. You will have to decide how deeply you want to explore this element.

SCENE

The choice of the "Scene" should not lead to the same degree of divergence. It is, of course, a television series in the United States in the first decade of the twenty-first century. You would likely add the audience as part of the "Scene" and Fox Television as a player. Fox has often been identified as the last major channel to appear in American television and as a channel with a different approach and a different demographic—arguably a younger demographic than the ones watching NBC, CBS, or ABC. Depending on how far you want to develop the "Scene," you might also include something about the American Dream, about separate support groups for separate contestants, about the financial dimensions behind a successful series, about the particular rewards given an *Idol* winner, and so on.

PURPOSE

Your choice of "Agent" will probably determine your comment on the "Purpose" of this "Act." One view sees the series as simply about profit, with FremantleMedia (19 Management) and Fox enjoying significant wealth as result of the popularity of the series. Thus 19 Management gets the fee for producing the series, the distributing rights to that series, and automatic contracts with all the contestants, including the winner. Fox gets the $710,000 per one-minute ad and other spinoffs.

A few contestants make significant money through the contracts they win as a result of their participation. Other contestants get contracts of lesser value even if they do not become the Idol. All the contestants who last through two rounds get valuable publicity and experience. So a case can be made that the "Purpose" is the opportunity offered the contestants.

It is harder but still possible to make a case for the audience being the "Purpose." The program could never have lasted so many years without a large audience to ensure high status and large financial returns. Obviously, the first reward for the audience is their attachment to a series that lasts many weeks coupled with their sense of direct participation (and influence) through the voting mechanism. You might even argue that the audience gets confirmation that the American Dream is alive and well,.

THE RATIOS

ACT-PURPOSE

Given the extent of the discussion already offered on the individual parts of the Pentad, there is no need to discuss this particular ratio beyond what has already been presented.

AGENT-PURPOSE

This relationship has already been explored. What we hope you discover through this prewriting technique is that applying the ratios forces you to explore relationships. If you see the "Agent" as being the players who most directly profit from the series financially, that will lead to one exploration here. If you see the "Agent" as being the audience, which profits in less concrete ways, but nevertheless profits, you will go a different direction with your analysis. And so on.

AGENCY-PURPOSE

Here again, the analysis of these terms separately should give you enough of a guide to check against your own discussion of this ratio. If you think the "Agency" equates to the ownership of the medium that produces the series and the medium that directly presents the series, your discussion will highlight the economic element—that is, the getting and investing of money. That may be the chief element if you look at the contestants as well, but you will probably also see that the performers get more than money for their time. For many of them, it is their fifteen minutes of fame. If you see the audience as the dominant "Agency," you will discuss other elements. In the case of the audience, the "Purpose" becomes more complex, probably extending beyond the simple level of entertainment. You may want to ask why the audience, initially, was so young. And you would be inclined to relate "Purpose" to both the dream of wealth and fame and the sense the audience receives of direct involvement in the process.

Exercise 2-2 Mind-Mapping

We believe that the answer key for Exercise 2-2 should give you enough background to guide your evaluation of your mind-mapping exercise. We assume that almost all of you will choose the *Idol* series as your central circled entry. What should be interesting when you look at your mind-mapping is what the first relationship was that you chose to explore—contestants, audience, or producer/broadcaster. Of equal interest will be the visual relationships your mapping creates for each of the key elements—first to your central term, and second to your other terms. Does your visual work reinforce your written work or does it produce new relationships and ideas?

You may wish to compare your work with the mapping done by another student. Do you think that a visual representation, such as the one provided by mind-mapping, is a more productive way for you to prewrite than the print-bound way represented by applying the Pentad? If so, you have learned something about the way your mind works in exploring what you know about a subject and what you may need to explore further.

The above comments also apply to the work you may have done in response to the OPTION part of the exercise.

Exercise 2-3 Applying Topic Analysis

This answer key will be shorter than it would have been had responses not already been provided that address the subject matter of the three topics supplied by this exercise. This should demonstrate that applying any one of the prewriting techniques should help you explore your subject in more depth than if you had simply written down random responses generated by the subject.

CIRCUMSTANCES SURROUNDING THE EVENT OR PROCESS

The intent of this topic is to force your mind to examine the context surrounding the event or process you are exploring. Here, the subject is both an event and a process. But it is easier to think of these terms interchangeably. Two of the contexts that should arise when you apply this topic are "reality show" and "television."

The term "reality show" is relatively recent and applies principally to the medium of television. The *Idol* series is clearly a reality show because such shows, by definition, do not rely on invented characters, plots, or dialogue. Instead, a "real" set of characters and a situation provide the base for the series. You may or may not know that one of the principal appeals of "reality shows" to their producers is the lower costs involved. There are no expensive actors and writers and directors and so on to pay. The second appeal of the "reality show" is the loyalty of its viewers. Most such shows involve a serially evolving circumstance. To this, the *Idol* series adds the participatory function of the voting mechanism. The second context here, "television," has already been discussed. It is a medium that is there to make a profit for its shareholders, and the chief means of profit is advertising revenue. That supplies one of the angles you have to consider when evaluating the *Idol* series. As mentioned before, the direct appeal to youth is also a feature here, as is the underlying influence of the "American Dream," the sudden shift of status from have-not to have.

Obviously, your analysis may go further, but the point of topic analysis is to apply fixed topics to a subject to see what doing so reveals. Take a look at what you have discovered.

WHO OR WHAT WAS AFFECTED BY THIS EVENT OR PROCESS?

This has been covered in previous sample answers. See what your application has revealed. Do you think the viewers are affected? We would probably all agree that the contestants have been affected. But what is the difference in effect for the successful and the unsuccessful candidate? Of all the "whats" affected, television is likely the one you didn't think about too much. Is it affected?

IS THE EVENT/PROCESS GOOD? BAD? BY WHOSE STANDARDS?

This topic is a tricky one, especially because it asks you to apply terms of value. That means you have to define what they mean to you. In a simple sense, no one is hurt by an entertainment program. In a more complex sense, what we watch does have some influence on how we perceive and respond to our world. Do you see anything to worry about as far as the *Idol* series is concerned? We do know that as many as one out of seven Americans watch this show, as do many Canadians. But to the majority of watchers it is simply entertainment. Is there any meaning behind the fact that, typically, there are more votes registered than watchers of the show?

As the topic makes clear, you are going to have to define the value terms you are asked to apply here. Perhaps the best test of the utility of this prewriting technique is whether you have discovered anything new about your subject by applying it.

TO WHAT OTHER EVENTS IS IT CONNECTED?

A case can be made that this show empowers its audience, engaging them at a deeper level than most entertainment shows do. That is a function, perhaps, of its asking viewers to pick a favourite and then support that favourite by voting. Perhaps one measure of how "real" some viewers find the show was the accusation, in the early years, that black contestants were not being given a fair shake. The loudest expression of this came in a year when a black singer was chosen Idol of the Year. What does that signify? Can this kind of voting have any influence on individuals voting in other contexts—say, an election? If so, why was the American turnout in 2004 so weak and in 2008 so much stronger? Can we even relate the show's voting to political voting?

You may have found somewhere to go with this topic. Equally, it may not have seemed a productive inquiry to you. You have to decide which prewriting techniques work for you and which don't.

Chapter 3 Prewriting III: Skill Development

Exercise 3-1 Applying Causal Analysis

The following answers are illustrative. There are many causes of the popularity of this show, so consider the ones we have supplied as suggestions only. The purpose of this exercise is to give you an opportunity to apply a thinking skill in a realistic frame. You should have discovered that using the different categories here has helped you discover and organize causes for a particular phenomenon before writing about them.

IMMEDIATE CAUSES

—The most obvious precipitating cause (another term for a special kind of immediate cause) is that Elizabeth Murdoch persuaded her father to disregard his experts and purchase the *Idol* franchise from its British producer as a summer replacement show in 2002.

—One of the immediate causes behind the quick acceptance of the show and its move from an initial ranking of 30th to eventual first place (in 2006) is the imprinting factor. The show is structured in a way that encourages viewers to "adopt" a contestant and become a supporter of that contestant. In this regard, the voting mechanism is a key element in promoting active support for a particular singer.

—Another immediate cause is the elimination process, which promotes active sponsorship of a contestant and has been a feature of the show since its inception. You may add the "judging" component here or give it separate status.

—Yet another feature linked to the elimination process is the structured use of an initial selection followed by a semifinal, a final, and a finale. This allows a five-month buildup of suspense, sponsorship, and attachment between viewer and contestant.

—You may observe that the show is aimed at a relatively young demographic—a feature that has been present since the show's beginning.

—The million-dollar contract awaiting the winner establishes an "instant wealth and fame" element that has special appeal to the audience.

INTERMEDIATE CAUSES

—Given the initial establishment of the show's distinctive features, the intermediate causes can focus on the refining of those features. One element that was refined over time was the creation of distinctive personas for the judges, ranging from the female airhead in love with every contestant to the acerbic Englishman who approves of practically no one and who has a distinctive way of communicating his disapproval. Applauding one judge and booing another is an opportunity for the live audience to participate actively. Furthermore, the television audience can agree or disagree with the live audience's reactions; in both cases, participation is enhanced by the judging feature. The importance of the judging element is underlined by the 2009 decision to add a fourth judge, thereby creating a balanced panel of two men and two women.

—The adoption of new technology has given the show a contemporary appeal. The texting of votes for a fee promotes the magical "participation"; it also has a special appeal to the young. One fact that demonstrates the special appeal of the voting feature is the presence of no more than 41 million viewers but as many as 65 million voters (or should we say votes).

—The tweaking of the structure—including the creation of veto and rescue rights for judges—is designed to heighten the tension and to retain favoured contestants for as long as possible, whether that contestant is particularly gifted or not.

—Special interest groups have added to the show's overall audience. This is indicated by such events as a protest made by black Americans, during the third season, that black contestants were not being judged fairly. Ironically, the eventual winner that season was a black American. This incident serves to remind us that special interest groups were created as a part of the *Idol* series' market penetration.

REMOTE CAUSES

—Perhaps the most influential remote cause is the way the show appeals directly to the "American Dream," that belief distinctive to American culture that anyone can be wealthy or famous or even President. The facts that demonstrate how incorrect, statistically, this belief is have no apparent impact on the public's acceptance of it. Clearly, the million-dollar contract and the fact that at least one contestant, Jordin Sparks, sold two-and-a-half million copies of her first recording after becoming a winner, suggest that the audience expects the *Idol* winner to be rewarded with immediate access to wealth and fame.

—Another cause that is remote and not widely known is the economic reward reaped by the show's producer and broadcaster. Fox has publicly acknowledged annual profits as high as $500 million. As well, 19 Management enjoys the worldwide broadcasting rights and signs every contestant to a 12- to 14-month contract and thereby garners a part of the wealth accruing from the Idols' recordings and appearances.

—A large part of Fox's revenue comes from advertising. American companies as diverse as Ford, AT&T, Coca-Cola, and Kellogg's have been with the show from the beginning. Clearly, these companies see their alliance with a leading television show as valuable, even though only AT&T profits directly from it. The $710,000 charged for a thirty-second commercial could be called a remote or immediate cause of the show's success. Also, most viewers don't realize how much cheaper a reality show is to produce than a fictional show, mainly because only a million dollars or so goes to "salaries" (i.e., for the show's stars).

NECESSARY CAUSES

—This is the first of the trickier groupings. By definition, a necessary cause is one that would be present in any list of causes. For that reason, we would include the high ranking of the *Idol* series because it is the top five ranking that establishes the cost of an advertising minute or thirty seconds. For that reason, the show's popularity is a necessary cause.

—You may choose to place the high revenue and low cost of the *Idol* programs as a separate necessary cause. Certainly, the program remains on Fox because of its high value to the company and its shareholders.

—An allied element here is the lower cost of producing a "reality show." This kind of show has significantly lower production costs, especially when you consider that the show was available for a simple purchase; the production costs had already been picked up by FremantleMedia. The financial attractiveness of the show is therefore attached to the ongoing costs as well as to the revenues it produces.

—We probably have to include the fact that 19 Management must make contact with the next generation of entertainers if it wishes to maintain its high ratings as an entertainment company. The production of the *Idol* series by a subsidiary company gave 19 Management the access to future stars that it needed. The shrewd part of the arrangement was that 19 Management retained contractual relationships with all those who auditioned. Just the relationship with the winner gave 19 Management access to a contractual share of revenues as high as $200 million for a successful album and hit songs.

—Now it gets more challenging. Is the appeal to a young demographic a necessary cause or not? A case can be made for that status, but another analysis might say it is not a necessary cause. Equally, can you make separate cases for the structure of the show and the way that structure captures and holds a significant audience? Is that a necessary cause or an important one?

—We are inclined to include the "American Dream" element as a necessary cause, but we realize that another analyst might see it as only contributory. And we could extend this difference of opinion to other causes we have cited.

SUFFICIENT CAUSE

—Basically, we write a causal analysis with the intention of capturing the cause or causes that must be included if we hope to establish the sufficient cause of a phenomenon or event—in this case, the phenomenon of the lasting popularity of the *American Idol* series. One of the simplest ways to begin is to include the precipitating cause—here, the persuasive powers of Elizabeth Murdoch in persuading her father to purchase a show that his experts did not recommend.

—Equally, we have to include the financial arrangements if we want to be sure we have identified sufficient cause. Those arrangements include the interests of FremantleMedia and its parent company, 19 Management; the revenues garnered by Fox for broadcasting a top-ranked show; and the attraction of the million-dollar recording prize pursued by the contestants.

—The structure of the show, with its progressive elimination feature and its highlighting of individual contestants, is probably also part of defining sufficient cause. Here you can include the attraction and retention of large audiences, the fascination with the contestant's chance to hit the "big time," and the appeal to specialized segments of the audience by different contestants.

—The show's longevity—eight years and counting—suggests that it has wide appeal. You may even want to include the unique feature of running the program only four months a year (approximately) as part of the *American Idol* series' strong appeal. Most fictional shows run seven months a year.

To capture the "sufficient cause" of this show's durable appeal to a large audience, it is probably enough to focus on how the show became popular, the monies that accrued to it because of its popularity, the special appeal to a young demographic, and its combination of regional and national appeal.

Exercise 3-2 Working with Inferences

The answers provided below are intended to be illustrative. They are the ones we had in mind when we composed this exercise. However, there are other answers that would satisfy the need for the inference to be logically a product of the two factual statements supplied. If you have any doubt about the validity of the inference you supplied, please check it with your instructor.

1. The change in earning power and living costs over those thirty years made it difficult to manage without both parents working.

    Alternatively, the belief that you should be able to buy a home and enjoy certain luxuries required incomes from both parents.

2. The greater return in profit available to those farmers growing corn for biofuels, together with the general shortage of available corn, caused the price of corn to rise.

3. Political circumstances changed so drastically as a result of the financial collapse of 2008–9 that budgets deficit were necessary because of lost tax revenues and economic stagnation.

4. The market for newspapers is getting weaker. More people are choosing to get their news from radio and television or from online sources. At least one of those online sources is the online edition of a newspaper.

5. In Canada, there has been no decline in readership of newspapers, but some readers now choose the online option for their news source.

6. *Inference One:* Despite the end of mandatory retirement in B.C., the percentage of people working past the age of 65 has not changed much.

Inference Two: The largest shift in workers continuing past 65 so far measured is the 70% of university professors who have passed 65 and continue to work. This suggests that their work is more attractive than the work of other public-sector employees or that they need the money more.

7. It follows that an employer's cost for labour will be higher if the proportion of older workers is higher. In the case of universities, therefore, the benefits and labour costs are higher than they would be if there were more workers not at the top of the salary scale.

8. The increase in the number of stores opened by Lee Valley Tools suggests a higher demand for that chain's goods. This may in turn reflect a general aging of the population and an increase in the number of retirees, when one considers that gardening, for instance, is a hobby of retired people. Or it may simply reflect an increase in the do-it-yourself and hobby markets.

9. *Inference One:* Universities must no longer need to determine whether an individual applicant should be admitted or not. This is emphasized by the fact that some postsecondary programs for which applicants outnumber positions continue to use differential admissions practices such as a student's Grade Twelve GPA.

    Inference Two: Because most Canadian universities no longer use marks for general admission purposes, there must have been a decline in the number of applicants for admission. A little research will show you that the Grade Twelve cohort in Canada has declined in number; this explains why there is no longer any general need for differential admission practices.

10. The increasing popularity of juices and energy drinks reflects the new realization that bottled water is an anti-environmental practice, given the need for oil derivatives in all the bottles manufactured to hold water. It may also be linked to health concerns related to plastics and food packaging. Ironically, it reflects the fact that a practice once seen as healthy for the individual is now seen as unhealthy for the environment and for the individual.

Exercise 3-3 Writing the Inference Paragraph

The following answer key discusses, in general terms, how you might have written the two sample paragraphs. In each case, the key relationship is between the facts and the generalization you draw from those facts. The placement of that generalization is not critical. However, putting the generalization first places more emphasis on the generalization. Putting it last places more emphasis on the process by which you arrived at the generalization. Accordingly, the notes below give some sample sets of facts and the generalizations you might draw from those facts.

FACTS

—The percentage of teens stating their faith as Catholic declined from 50% to 18% between 1984 and 2008, a decline of over one-third.

—The percentage of teens stating their faith as Protestant declined from 35% to 13% between 1984 and 2008, a decline of slightly less than one-third.

—The percentage of teens stating their faith as "other" increased from 3% to 16% between 1984 and 2008, a fivefold increase.

—The percentage of teens stating their faith as "no faith" increased from 12% to 32% between 1984 and 2008, almost a threefold increase.

—The two largest groups in the 2008 survey, both equalling 32% of respondents, were the Catholic and "no faith" groups.

—In 1984, 85% of respondents identified their faith as Catholic or Protestant; the 2008 survey saw this total decline to 45%.

—The respondents identifying themselves as "other faiths" and "no faith" constituted about half the respondents in 2008, compared to 15% in 1984.

—The largest shift in the four surveys occurred in the 1992 survey in comparison to the 1984 survey, a shift among the four categories of 32%.

—The largest percentage shift over the four surveys occurred in the "no faiths" group.

POSSIBLE INFERENCES

—It appears that the faiths once seen as central to Canadian culture have seen the biggest decline among teens in this survey, which has been conducted every eight years since 1984.

—The data suggest that the decline in teens declaring themselves as Catholic and Protestant has not led to an equal increase in those professing "other faiths."

—The data clearly indicate that a loss of faith of any kind is one of the two central trends unearthed by these surveys.

—Further study of the data documenting declining percentages of teens stating a faith in the Catholic and Protestant religions might point to a change in the composition of the Canadian population over the 24 years surveyed. This would require additional research.

—The 2016 survey will show a further shift away from the Catholic and Protestant categories.

—The 2016 survey will show an increase in those respondents who say they have no faith.

Sample Paragraph #1

The major trend that emerges from the four surveys of teens on their beliefs conducted by Project Teen is the decline of expressed belief in the Catholic and Protestant churches. In the 1984 survey, 85% of respondents expressed their belief in one of these two faiths, with the Catholic choice earning 50% of total responses by itself. The most recent survey, published in 2008, shows that only 45% of respondents identified themselves as Catholic or Protestant, with the Protestant choice gaining only 13% agreement. While "other faiths" showed growth over the same time frame, increasing by 13%, the major gain was in the number of teens expressing "no Faith," 32%.

Sample Paragraph #2

Project Teen has now done four surveys of a sample of teens to ascertain their beliefs. The first was in 1984, the last in 2008. In the first, 85% of the respondents chose to identify themselves as either Catholic or Protestant, with 50% of those choosing Catholic. By 1992, that number was 69% (39% Catholic), and, by 2000, 61% (39% Catholic). The most recent survey shows 32% of respondents identifying their belief as Catholic and 13% as Protestant. Clearly, a major trend in these successive surveys is the decline in the number of participants who state they are Catholic or Protestant—a number that has virtually been cut in half over the twenty-four years that the survey has been conducted. Logic suggests that this number will shrink again in the 2016 survey.

Exercises 3-4 and 3-5 Working with Synthesis

Exercise 3-4 Definition

DEFINITION: Identify the class to which the term to be defined belongs.

Most answers will begin by defining the class as "television shows." Following that, they will specify a smaller class, "reality shows." They may go ahead and suggest that these shows have been popular for well over a decade and that several of them, including the two mentioned here, have consistently ranked high in terms of audience size. They may also include the fact that these shows feature "real" people responding to challenges, often with a cash prize for the most successful participant. However, they will have identified the class once they say "reality shows."

DEFINITION (ctd.): Use contrast to develop your definition.

The following list is, again, a suggestion. You may well have chosen different ways to distinguish these two types of shows.

1. A "fictional show," whether a comedy or a drama, has a script written by professional writers and timed to provide a fifty-two-minute hour or twenty-six minute half-hour. A reality show has a structure for its hour (or longer), but the "outcome" is not limited to a script.
2. A "fictional show" carries a large budget to pay for its actors, its writers, its directors and producers, and its technical crew. Some individual actors receive a million dollars or more for a single show. A "reality show" has a much smaller budget to pay for its set or sets, the travel and lodging of its participants, and the production and direction involved in its presentation. Generally, the budget for a reality show is much smaller than for a "fictional show."
3. A fictional show can limit its plot to one episode or carry it forward over two or more episodes. The "plot" of a "reality show" takes the whole season to reach its climax.
4. The plots of "reality shows" are generally limited to the resolution of a competition, with a reward for the "champion." "Fictional shows" have a much larger repertoire of plots to employ.
5. A "fictional show" may choose to carry over its characters from season to season. A "reality show" generally starts each new season with a new cast of players.
6. Many "fictional shows" employ standard plot devices such as the "hook" at the beginning (before the commercial), and the "tease" at the end. "Reality shows" employ certain standard devices, but they are not similar to the devices of the "fictional show."
7. The most recurring structural feature of the "reality show" is the competition. This is not used in any overt way by most "fictional shows."
8. "Reality shows" have different means by which to actively involve their viewers in the results of the action. One means is allowing the audience to vote.

DEFINITION (ctd.): Use comparison to develop your definition.

Using comparison, you can summarize common characteristics of reality shows. The following are possible characteristics.

1. A simple place to start is the element that attracts the most producers and broadcasters. The "reality show" has a significantly smaller budget than do "fictional shows." The absence of year-long salary liabilities to actors, directors, scenery production crews, and a long list of other employees is a real attraction to the broadcaster, whether it buys the show from an independent producer or handles the production itself.
2. The underlying structure of most "reality shows" is the competition, during which multiple contestants attempt to win the grand prize. The "competitors" can be individuals, duos, even teams.
3. Along with the structural contribution of the contest is the use of voting. That voting can be conducted exclusively among judges or contestants, or it can be extended to the public viewers of the show, as in the case of *American Idol*.
4. These shows rely on an "imprinting" on the public of favoured contestants. The "reality show" uses a progressive elimination but is careful to retain many contestants for as long as possible. The *Idol* series even gives a judge the right to bring back a contestant. The point is that segments of the viewing public adopt favourites and use voting and other means to advance the status of the favourite. "Reality shows" understand the power of imprinting when it comes to establishing and retaining an audience that wants to see its favourite succeed. The "survival reality shows" even have columnists in newspapers discussing the possible success or failure of individual members of the "tribes."
5. The "reality show" cultivates the appearance of being broadcast "live," whether the show has been taped and shaped or not. This establishes an illusion of immediacy that is part of the appeal of such shows.
6. Though this is not true of all "reality shows," many of them make deliberate use of exotic locales as an additional appeal. *The Amazing Race* and *Survival* are examples of this.
7. "Reality shows" use the appeal of a contestant becoming rich or famous (or both) as another means of building and retaining an audience.
8. One key to the success of the "reality shows" has been the high ratings that so many have managed to gain. High ratings increase the cost of a 30- or 60-second commercial to an advertiser and therefore enhance the profit that a broadcaster can make from this kind of show. When you couple this with the lower cost of creating such shows, you can see the financial advantage to broadcasters like Fox and CBS.

SUMMARY OF DEFINITION

We don't need to repeat what has already been said. Basically, however, you create your overall definition by combining the "class" you placed your term into with the distinguishing characteristics you selected from the work you have done, using contrast and comparison as your thinking aids. Whether you have used most of the characteristics we have included here or only a few doesn't matter. What you should learn from this exercise is how to use the thinking skill called *definition* as an assist to any essay you write. Many of the essays you are assigned in your postsecondary classes will require you to do some preliminary definitional work.

Exercise 3-5 Creating a Synthesis

As usual with this kind of exercise, it is impossible to provide a single response that will suit each student's approach. What we have provided, therefore, is an illustrative answer.

Paragraph #1

In this paragraph, you might well focus on the history of the "reality show"—on the pioneering shows that came out in the last half of the 1990s—and begin to establish the template for this kind of show. Perhaps you will choose to emphasize the role of the contest in these shows, demonstrated so well by the *Survival* shows, which have deliberately reverted to what seems a much older time, with "tribes," "alliances," "exotic" surroundings, and contestants being "voted off the island." Perhaps you will show how some of these elements have been adapted by *American Idol* and *The Amazing Race*. Certainly, sketching a history of "reality shows" and the characteristics developed by those shows will be enough to fill a paragraph.

Paragraph #2

If you want to do a paragraph on the financial dimension of *American Idol* and *The Amazing Race*, you have plenty of material. One place to start is the combined impact of low costs for the show and high financial returns through advertising. You can use specific numbers, such as the $720,000 per 60-second commercial that the *Idol* series has been able to attract, the enormous viewing and voting audiences of the *Idol* series (an audience of up to 41 million viewers and a vote that once numbered 65 million), the seven Emmys won by CBS's *The Amazing Race* and what that network did to gather an audience for the show, and so on. In the land of television, shows survive mainly because they attract and retain an audience; this is more important than the critics' respect.

Paragraph #3

You could write an interesting paragraph on the role of the competition in these two shows and how this aspect is developed through the structure and details of each show. Regarding *American Idol*, you have unique elements such as the audience's vote, the role and developed character of the judging panel, the extension of vetoes to the individual judges, the successive trimming of the number of contestants, and the use of a finale following the final. Moving to *The Amazing Race*, you have the appeal of each individual show in the series. Each show creates suspense through a race among all the teams to reach the Check-In Mat before at least one other team (with the exception of the last two races). *The Amazing Race* also uses the additional suspense of a progressive elimination to hold its audience. You could, in fact, easily write two paragraphs on this dimension of the two shows.

Paragraphs #4, #5, etc.

Again, you can see how easy it would be to write more paragraphs exploring the common facets of the two shows. You should probably reserve your final paragraph for a summary of the major points of your synthesis. This exercise has given you the experience of constructing a synthesis by starting with a definition and common characteristics to provide you with the material necessary for evaluating the common dimensions in the two shows.

Part II ACADEMIC WRITING

Chapter 9 Summary

Exercise 9-1 The Summary

The following are the key elements of the passage you should include in a summary. Of course, there are different ways of combining these elements. Following the underlined passage, you will find one suggestion.

The underlined key points can be used in a summary

In his book *On Equilibrium,* John Ralston Saul comments that people have forgotten to use common sense when dealing with social problems. Instead of dealing with poverty or homelessness by looking at their underlying causes and working to eliminate them, we only examine the data on poverty and homelessness and react to issues when there is a spike in the number of people affected. In other words, we are reactive, not proactive. We react to suppress the dramatic rise of a problem. When the crisis declines, we move on to reacting to other urgent problems that are conspicuously above the norm. As a result, we do not abide by a set of social principles that we believe are fundamental to the rights of every member of society.

Saul suggests we have gone back to mid-nineteenth-century moralism and its views on people in distress. Moralism, according to Saul, reinforces the divisions between the people who hold power and wealth and those who do not. It asserts the right of those in power to feel good about charitable donations for those in misery. This method of helping underprivileged people is reflected in infomercials on television that appeal to viewers to support children in developing countries by making a personal and financial contribution to a child's development. These appeals strengthen their case by noting that people who donate will receive a photograph of the child they are supporting and get progress letters from the child to show how sponsors' donations are helping. The appeal and the support becomes personal, the link between those supporting the charity and the individuals being supported tangible. In this method of funding, those who can afford to help get to feel good about doing so; those who are supported get to thank those who support them, but the underlying problems are not examined, let alone solved.

Sadly, according to Saul, in a world bereft of common sense, more and more individuals become marginalized, and more and more people need food banks and charity to lead, not normal, but impoverished lives. Common sense suggests that, as a society, we should be working to ensure people are not marginalized. We should be examining the underlying problems of poverty and homelessness and working to eliminate them so that we don't have to spend endless amounts of money dealing with outcomes that can be avoided. We should not have to have a part of the population feeling good about its wealth to the point where it feels good about supporting those that society fails, those who cannot afford to live normal lives. Something is dreadfully wrong with society when an elite portion of society feels good about supporting an underprivileged underclass.

The poorest federal riding in Canada, the Vancouver Downtown Eastside, has, for years, presented a problem of abject poverty mixed with drug and alcohol problems. Every year, politicians argue about how to deal with homelessness, alcoholism, drug use, and prostitution in this riding; every year, millions of dollars are spent on projects that do not eliminate the poverty creating these issues, but, instead, treat the symptoms manifested by those trapped in poverty. Can society afford to continue ignoring the plight of such people and still see itself as humane? In his book, Saul remarks, "What common sense provides is a clear sense that nothing is inevitable; that we belong to a society" (64). What Saul is pointing out is that people often forget they are a part of a greater whole rather than isolated from it and its problems.

Summary from the key points

In *On Equilibrium*, John Ralston Saul remarks that we do not use common sense to solve social problems by finding their causes. Instead, we look at the data problems generate and react to problems when the size of the problem increases. Society is not proactive; it reacts to problems only when they become excessive. Our attitudes reflect nineteenth-century moralism; we value those who show moral good by giving charity to those in need. Because of our lack of common sense, more of society is falling to the margins, unable to live decent lives. We need to work to help those in need and examine and eliminate underlying problems that cause marginalization. How can we see ourselves as humane if we do not? We need to be a part of society, instead of isolating ourselves from society's problems.

Words: 138/588 = 23.5% of the original length

Part IV DOCUMENTATION

Chapter 21 Avoiding Plagiarism

Exercise 21-1 Plagiarism: The Essentials

After each answer, you will find an explanation that will help you understand plagiarism more fully. If you are still confused, please refer to your handbook for more help.

1. If I find something on the Web, it is obviously in the public domain, and I don't have to cite my source.
Wrong Items on the Web have to be treated as you would any source of information. Make sure you cite the source of any quotation and include the source in your bibliography, too.

2. There is no author listed on the website, so students can cut and paste sentences or even short passages into their essay without showing that they got the material from the Web.
Wrong Check your handbook for how to deal with a source that has no author. MLA, APA, CSE, Chicago, and Columbia Online all make allowances for how to cite a source that has no evident author. As online sites do not always indicate who authored a work, you may have to cite the organization responsible for the publication or the site, or you may have to cite your source by its title.

3. If I can find the same information in a variety of newspaper, radio, television, and online sources, I don't have to cite where I got the information.
Correct As the same information is available in a number of places, it is considered to be common knowledge. Common knowledge does not need to be cited.

4. Two people can work together and share their work and not have to worry about plagiarism.

Wrong Unless your instructor has indicated that you may work with someone else and hand in a joint essay, you should not share your work with someone else. You could both be accused of plagiarism and receive a zero for the assignment. If you are ever unsure of what is acceptable, ask your instructor. Otherwise, assume that you are not allowed to share your work with another student.

5. Encyclopaedias do not have to be sited either in the text of my essay or my bibliography.

Wrong Encyclopaedias should be cited. Quite a number of encyclopaedias list the author for each entry. Treat all work from these kinds of reference books as you would any other source.

6. I have a friend who took the same course last semester. I asked her if I could look at her paper and draw ideas from it. I don't have to worry about plagiarism as she said I could use her paper.

Wrong Any material you use needs to be cited. You may be putting yourself in grave danger of receiving a zero for an assignment if you use material from a paper that has already been submitted for a grade.

7. If I just use a phrase from a website or a book, that is plagiarism.

Correct Any borrowing of specific information or specific phrasing is plagiarism. Make sure you cite anything you borrow.

8. If I list the material I have looked at and used in writing my essay in my bibliography, I should still worry about plagiarism.

Correct You still must treat any direct quotations as borrowings and cite them in the body of your paper. As well, any paraphrase in the text of your essay that utilizes specific information should be cited.

9. The tutor in the learning centre helped strengthen my writing and straighten out some of my ideas, but that is not a problem.

Wrong Tutors in learning centres usually have strict rules that forbid them from helping students with ungraded papers. If you are unsure, ask your instructor so that you know what is acceptable practice and what is not. Do not allow someone to edit your work before you hand it in to be graded unless your instructor gives you permission to do so. You may, of course, get someone to review your work after it has been graded so that you understand the errors you made.

10. I cited my quotation on the first page, and it is clear that my second quotation (on page four) is from the same source, but I still have to cite my second quotation.

Correct You must cite every borrowing.

11. If I am using a source that generally is relating common knowledge, then specific information that is not necessarily found in three or more sources does not have to be cited.

Wrong Even though your source is using common knowledge, the moment it uses specific knowledge that you cannot find in three or more sources, you must cite the source.

12. A summary does not need to be cited. After all, it is in my own words, not the author's.

Wrong Even if you use your words to state someone's idea, you must give credit for the borrowing.

13. I took notes in class. I am going to use the exact words of my instructor. I should cite him and the date of the class in my essay.

Correct Any borrowing should be cited. You may wish to talk to your instructor about this, though.

14. Wikipedia is jointly authored by people who use the site. As such, there is no author and I don't have to cite any borrowings from the site.

Wrong You should cite material from Wikipedia just as you would cite information from any website. Some instructors may not want you to use sites like Wikipedia, though, as not everyone considers the material on this site reliable. Besides this, entries on Wikipedia are prone to change, and your instructor may criticize the site as not being a stable source of information.

Exercise 21-2 Plagiarism: Knowing What to Avoid

In the following passage, the problems have been struck out, and the remedies have been bolded after each error. Comments on the errors have been added in a smaller font between the lines of the essay.

Many postsecondary students have read either George Orwell's *Animal Farm* or

1984 in high school and understand that, in these books, Orwell was criticizing the state

of Europe in the period immediately following WW II. But Orwell's writing had its roots

in the fact that he was a ~~democratic socialist, a member of the Independent Labour~~

~~Party,~~ **"democratic socialist and a member of the Independent Labour Party"; he was**
This is a direct quotation and must be set off as a quotation and be followed by a parenthetic reference
strongly critical of the leadership of ~~Joseph Stalin and was suspicious of Moscow-~~

~~directed Stalinism~~ **"Joseph Stalin and was suspicious of Moscow-directed Stalinism"**

(Wikipedia). It shouldn't be surprising that Orwell's *Animal Farm* did not come into print

Answer Key 177

without some problems. Its publication history is curiously affected by the politics Orwell was critical of. The book's original publisher, Jonathan Cape, backed out of publishing Orwell's book ~~due to the influence of Peter Smollett, who worked at the Ministry of~~

> This is a direct quotation. It may be common knowledge and found in three or more places, but because it is taken word for word from the original, it must be treated like a quotation and have a reference. (The reference could be handled by adding a tag at the beginning of the sentence "According to Wikipedia" if you wish to avoid a parenthetic reference). Remember, if you could find the information in three or more places, as long as you did not use a direct quotation, you would not have to include a reference.
>
> Most styles also suggest, where possible, that you source the origin of the information. In this case, *Wikipedia* does cite the source of its comments on the publication of *Animal Farm*, and you should make every attempt to look at the original source and, where appropriate, cite it and include it in your Works Cited.

~~Information~~ **"due to the influence of Peter Smollett, who worked at the Ministry of. Information"(Wikipedia).** Smollett, it later turned out, was [~~spying~~] **spying** for the

> The fact that Smollett was a spy is common knowledge. As such, it does not need a reference, even though the information was taken from the same source as the other statement about Smollett.

[~~USSR~~] **USSR** and obviously did not want Orwell's book, which he felt was critical of the Soviet Union, to be published. It was one year after the planned publication date that another publisher finally published *Animal Farm*.

Orwell's critical view of dictatorial states is again in evidence in *1984*, where, **Stephen Ingle suggests**, Orwell advises his readers that ~~the only possible constraint upon a totalitarian regime~~ **"the only possible constraint upon a totalitarian regime"**

> The two struck out statements are direct quotations from Ingle's article. The statements need to be treated as quotations and a reference needs to be added.

arises when an individual passes ~~judgements upon the nature of external reality~~ **"judgements upon the nature of external reality" (733).** Orwell is aware that individuals are ultimately responsible for regimes. He holds the position that there is no neutral ground. A non-response condones the acts of a regime just as much as willing participation in the acts of a regime. No one can hold a neutral ground; everyone is responsible for the acts of the state and for tyranny. Even though Orwell took the position that there is no such thing as a neutral stance in a tyrannical society, it is easy to see that people in such societies could feel they were faced with ~~a dilemma~~

<blockquote>Again, as this is a word-for-word quotation, it must be treated as such and have a reference.</blockquote>

~~from which there is no legal escape~~ "**a dilemma from which there is no legal escape**"

(**Wikipedia**). They would be damned by their society if they did not follow orders, and damned by others if they followed orders and took part in an atrocity against a group of people.

Orwell's criticism of the middle of the twentieth century dates back to the period before WWII, as his novel *Coming Up For Air,* which was first published in June 1939, three months before Britain's declaration of war in September 1939, demonstrates. In that novel, Orwell's narrator foresees a horrific future:

<blockquote>The following quotation, though from a website, needs to have a reference. As the website the material was taken from does not contain pagination, all you need do in your parenthetic citation is cite the website.</blockquote>

> All the things you've got at the back of your mind, the things you're terrified of, the things that you tell yourself are just a nightmare or only happen in foreign countries. The bombs, the food-queues, the rubber truncheons, the barbed wire, the coloured shirts, the slogans, the enormous faces, the machine-guns squirting out of bedroom windows. It's all going to happen. (***The Complete Works of George Orwell***)

Coming Up for Air was not the only work that Orwell published in 1939 that warned of impending war and social chaos. His essay "Marrakech" not only foresees the cataclysm of war on the horizon but also points to underlying causes of many of the conflicts that would create social discord in the world for the next fifty years. At the end of his essay, while observing a column of Senegalese French Army soldiers marching past, he asks the question "How much longer can we go on kidding these people? How long before they turn their guns in the other direction?" (234). Here, not only is Orwell seeing the movement toward world war, but he is also making his readers aware of the problems that lurk just below the surface of the colonial empires that had developed in the nineteenth century. In fact, "~~Marrakech" is a morality play, and *Orwell* forces us to see~~

<small>This is a direct quotation and must be treated as such and be followed by a reference</small>

"Marrakech' is a morality play, and *Orwell* forces us to see" the poverty and problems of colonial empires and feel ~~his moral indignation~~ **"his moral indignation" (March 163).**

Note: The following items had to be added to the Works Cited. They had not included in the original bibliography:

"Animal Farm." *Wikipedia.* Web. 1 May 2009.

Ash, Timothy Garton. "Orwell's List.*" The New York Review of Books.* 25 Sept. 2003. Web. 5 May 2009.

"George Orwell." *Wikipedia.* Web. 1 May 2009.

March, Thomas. "Orwell's 'Marrakech.'" *Explicator*, 57.3 (1999) *Academic Search Premier.* Web. 3 May 2009.

"Nuremberg Defense." Wikipedia. Web. 4 May 2009.

Works Cited

"*Animal Farm.*" *Wikipedia*. Web. 1 May 2009.

Ash, Timothy Garton. "Orwell's List.*" The New York Review of Books*. 25 Sept. 2003. Web. 5 May 2009.

"George Orwell." *Wikipedia*. Web. 1 May 2009.

Ingle, Stephen. "Lies, Damned Lies and Literature: George Orwell and 'The Truth'." *British Journal of Politics & International Relations*, 9.4 (2007): 730-746. Academic Search Premier. Web. 3 May 2009.

March, Thomas. "Orwell's 'Marrakech.'" *Explicator*, 57.3 (1999): 163-64. *Academic Search Premier*. Web. 3 May 2009.

"Nuremberg Defense." Wikipedia. Web. 4 May 2009.

Orwell, George. *Coming Up for Air. The Complete Works of George Orwell.* n. pag. Web. 5 May 2009.

---. "Marrakech." *The Nelson Introduction to Literature*. Ed. Al Valleau and Jack Finnbogason. Toronto: Nelson, 2004. 230-234.

***A warning about websites and how they can change quickly. The quotation on *Animal Farm* from Wikipedia disappeared the day after it was sourced. Popular websites like Wikipedia may be convenient, but they are prone to change and may not be the best or the most stable source of information.

Chapters 22–25 MLA, APA, Chicago, and Columbia Online Styles

Exercise 22-1, MLA, APA, Chicago, and Columbia Online Styles

If, after you review the exercise, you feel you need to review one of the styles, please reread Chapters 22 to 25 as needed.

1. b) Finnbogason, Jack and Al Valleau. *A Canadian Writer's Guide*. 4th ed. Toronto: Nelson, 2009. Print.

2. d) March, Thomas. "Orwell's 'Marrakech.'" *Explicator*, 57.3 (1999): 163-64. *Academic Search Premier*. Web. 3 May 2009.

3. c) italicized.

4. e) either c or d is correct.

5 c) Electronic Version.

6. c) add the URL, breaking the URL after a period or a slash.

7. b) italicized.

8. b) (accessed June 4, 2009).

9. a) italicized.

10. b) adding a URL, making breaks between any punctuation or slash if necessary.

11. e) Both c and d are correct. The date of access is not indicated in a citation unless the data is time-sensitive or the resource is not stable. If it is, the date of access is included by adding "(accessed June 4, 2009)" after the URL.

Answer Key 181

12. c) double-spaced in both electronic and print submissions, but electronic submissions do not indent any of the lines of the entries and place two blank lines between each entry.

13. c) is indicated at the end of the entry by adding (4 June 2009).

14. a) the name of the Blog/Chat/Moo added after the author's name, the title, and the date of the posting.

Part V BASIC GRAMMAR

Chapter 27 Parts of Speech

Exercise 27-1 Identifying Parts of Speech

1. The code **1 = noun, 2 = pronoun, 3 = verb, 4 = adverb** has been used to identify the nouns, pronouns, verbs, and adverbs in the following sentences.

    a) Many problems(1) associated with the production(1) and distribution(1) of food(1) have(3) recently(4) been(3) recognized.
    b) One of the largest issues(1) is(3) the volume(1) of water(1) required to produce food(1).
    c) For instance, it(2) takes(3) four pounds(1) of water to produce one pound(1) of beef.
    d) A pound(1) of grain(1), however, can(3) be(3) grown(3) with only one pound(1) of water(1).
    e) If we(2) all consumed(3) grain(1) as our principal food(1), we(2) would quickly(4) reduce(3) the amount(1) of water(1) we(2) need(3).
    f) However, the direction(1) that food production(1) is(3) taking is(3) the opposite(1) of what it(2) should be(3).
    g) As large new middle classes(1) are(3) created(3) in countries(1) like India(1) and China(1), the demand(1) for meat(1) increases(3).
    h) People(1) who(2) have(3) a larger income(1) feel(3) they(2) are(3) entitled to increase(3) the amount(1) of meat(1) in their(2) diet(1).
    i) If we(2) had(3) an unending supply(1) of water(1), this shift(1) would(3) not be(3) a problem(1).
    j) But the fact(1) is(3) that we(2) are(3) rapidly(4) depleting(3) our(2) water supply(1) in North America(1) and elsewhere(1).

182   Answer Key

2. The code **1 = adjective, 2 = adverb, 3 = conjunction, 4 = preposition, 5 = article** has been used to identify the adjectives, adverbs, conjunctions, prepositions, and articles.

a) A(5) second(1) aspect of(4) the rise in(4) food prices on(4) a(5) world-wide(1) basis is the(5) shifting(1) value of(4) corn.

b) Where(3) corn was once grown principally(2) for(2) food, whether(3) it was eaten by(4) livestock or humans, it is increasingly(2) grown as(4) an alternative(1) source of(4) fuel for(4) vehicles.

c) The American Midwest was once a(5) major(1) supplier of(4) food for(4) humans.

d) Now, more(1) and more(4) land is set aside to grow corn as(4) a(5) bio-fuel, a(5) cheap alternative for(4) oil.

e) On(4) the(5) surface, such a(5) change might seem to be a(5) prudent decision.

f) However, an unintended(1) result is the(5) increase of(4) the(5) value of(4) land now that it can produce an(5) alternative to(4) oil costing a(5) hundred dollars a(5) barrel or(5) more.

g) As(4) the(5) land's cost increases, the(5) farmer is reluctant to devote it to growing cattle(5) corn.

h) This means a(5) rise in(4) the(5) cost of(4) beef and other(1) livestock, one of the staple(1 foods consumed in(4) North America.

i) We also know now(2) that(3) the(5) energy necessary to convert corn to(4) ethanol, a(5) fuel, is significant, so(3) the contribution to reducing our dependency on(4) oil is not as(4) great as(4) we had hoped it would be.

j) As(4) in(4) other matters, we learn that(3) an(5) apparently(1) simple(1) cause turns out to be complex, and the(5) wish to do a(5) good thing about(4) our energy(1) use creates more harm than(3) we had anticipated.

3. The code **1 = noun, 2 = pronoun, 3 = verb, 4 = adjective, 5 = adverb, 6 = conjunction, 7 = preposition** has been used to identify the nouns, pronouns, verbs, adjectives, adverbs, conjunctions, and prepositions.

a) The costs(1) of(7) energy(1) are(3) a hidden(4) but(6) major(4) contributor(1) to(7) the cost(1) of(7) food(1) in(7) all(4) major(4) areas(1) of(7) the world(1), whether(6) that food(1) be grain(1) or(7) rice(1), beef(1) or(7) fish(1).

b) When(6) the price(1) of(7) oil(1) increases by(7) 50 %(1) in(7) the space(1) of(7) six(4) months(1), the world's(4) food(4) markets are(3) affected.

c) The fuel(1) used(3) by(7) tractors to plough(3) the earth(1), by(7) trucks(1), ships(1), and trains(1) to deliver(3) food(1) to(7) market(1) becomes(3) a much(4) larger(4) cost(1) to(7) the producer(10 and consumer(1).

d) The end(4) result(1) is(3) that(6) a world-wide(4) food(4) crisis(1) is(3) created.

e) If you(2) add in the effect(1) of(7) a tragic(4) typhoon(1) in(7) Burma/Myanmar(1), then(6) a particular(4) market(1) like(7) rice(1) is(3) doubly(5) affected.

f) The rice(4) bowl(1) of Asia(1), Burma/Myanmar(1) and Vietnam(1), have(3) both suffered(3) major(4) rice(4) crop(4) failures that(3) will(3) create(3) a shortage(1) of(7) a staple(4) Asian(4) food(1) and(6) raise(3) prices(1).

g) Unfortunately, this form(1) of(7) price(4) inflation(1) in(7) food(4) costs(1) comes(3) at(7) a time(1) when(6) the world(4) economy(1) has(3) suffered(3) a decline(1) because of(7) mortgage(4) collapses(1) in(7) the United(4) States(1) and the threat(1) of(7) recession(7) elsewhere(1).

h) This kind(1) of(7) development(1) reminds(3) us(2) of(7) how(4) intricately(5) the world's(4) markets(1) are(3) linked.

i) The escalation(1) of(7) prices(1) for(7) wheat(1), rice(1), corn(1), beef(1), and pork(1) caused by(7) nature(1) and by(7) humans hurts(3) most of(7) us(2) eventually(5).

j) If(6) we(2), at(7) the same(4) time(1), are(3) struggling(3) to pay off or(6) qualify for a mortgage(1), the pain(1) we(2) feel(3) will be(3) intensified.

Chapter 28 Phrases and Clauses

Exercise 28-1 Prepositional Phrases

The following passage includes a number of prepositional phrases. The phrases are underlined. The type of phrase is indicated above the phrase.

    adv   adj   adj   adj
For most Canadians, a trip across Canada is one of the essential ways of coming

   Adj   adj
to terms with the complexity of the country and its people. Canada is a broad, vast land,

      adv   adj
and it is composed of distinct regions that have distinct cultures with different attitudes. It

           adj   adj
would be wrong to make a generalization about the people of Canada, despite what

           adv   adj   adj
politicians would like Canadians to think. From the east coast of Canada in

     adv   adj
Newfoundland, to the west coast of British Columbia, Canada's geography and people,

         adv   adj

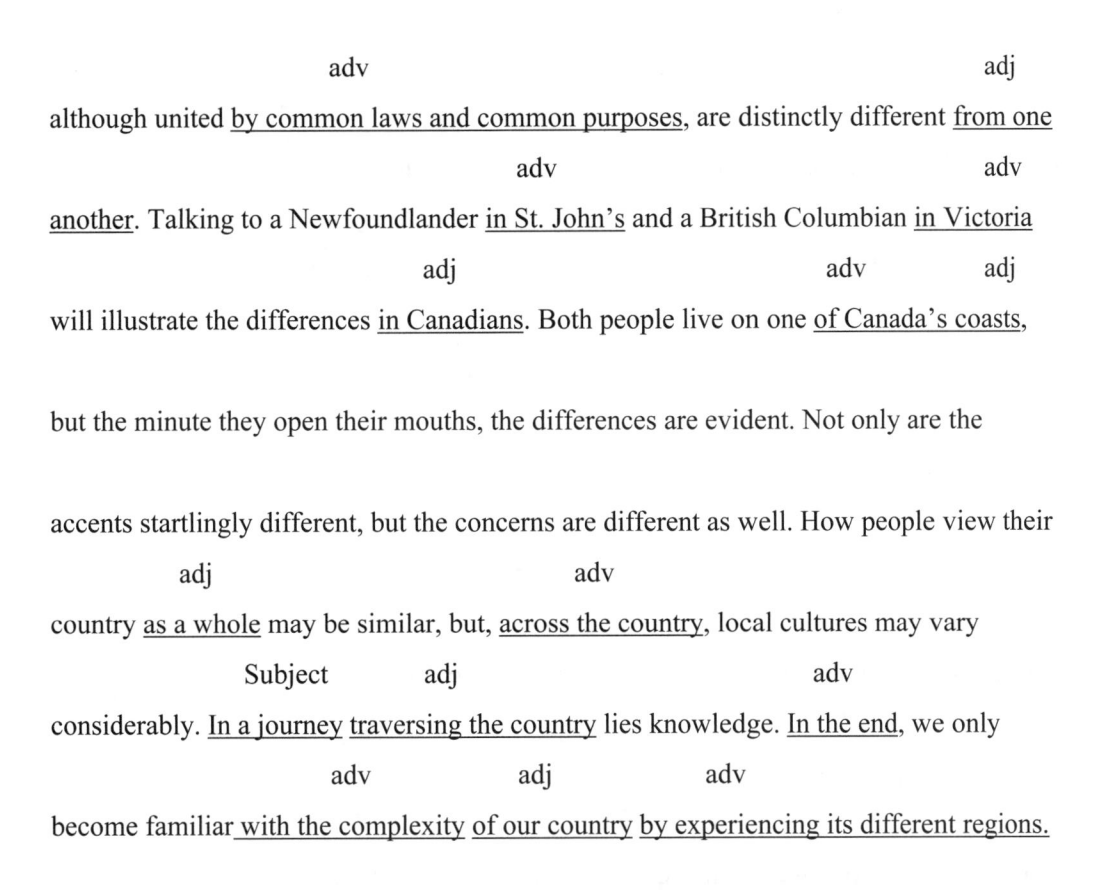

although united <u>by common laws and common purposes</u>, are distinctly different <u>from one

           adv   adv

another</u>. Talking to a Newfoundlander <u>in St. John's</u> and a British Columbian <u>in Victoria</u>

        adj   adv   adj

will illustrate the differences <u>in Canadians</u>. Both people live on one <u>of Canada's coasts</u>,

but the minute they open their mouths, the differences are evident. Not only are the

accents startlingly different, but the concerns are different as well. How people view their

    adj   adv

country <u>as a whole</u> may be similar, but, <u>across the country</u>, local cultures may vary

    Subject   adj   adv

considerably. <u>In a journey</u> <u>traversing the country</u> lies knowledge. <u>In the end</u>, we only

       adv   adj   adv

become familiar <u>with the complexity</u> <u>of our country</u> <u>by experiencing its different regions.</u>

Exercise 28-2 Participial, gerundial, and infinitive phrases

In the following passage, the participial, gerundial, and infinitive phrases are underlined and numbered according to whether the phrases are acting as adjectives, adverbs, or nouns.

  P = participial   *adjective = 1*

  G = Gerundial   *adverb = 2*

  I = Infinitive   *noun = 3*

   G-3   I-1

<u>Crossing the country</u> by car is one way <u>to notice</u> the geographical and cultural

        G-3

differences of the country. <u>Touring by car</u> has become a vacation pastime in North

               I-2

America, and it certainly is one of the major ways that Canadians come <u>to appreciate</u> the

      I-3   I-3   P-2

different parts of their country. <u>To see</u> Niagara Falls is <u>to experience</u> its enormity. See<u>ing</u>

the Rocky Mountains in the distance from Calgary, we can understand the sharp contrast they make with the western Canadian prairies. Gone are the days when people on one coast never saw the other coast or the land in between. Now, the outstanding sights of every region are a part of every Canadians' perspective on their country. <u>Walking the</u> (P-1) <u>streets</u> of Victoria's Chinatown <u>to observe</u> (I-1) the community, people will quickly realize they are in the midst of the oldest Chinese community in the country. <u>Seeing the old</u> (G-3) <u>buildings</u> (I-3) is in itself a treat, but the old buildings allow us <u>to visualize</u> (G-3) the complex history of the community. <u>Seeing our history</u> (G-3) and <u>understanding its intricacy</u> (G-3) permit us <u>to appreciate</u> (I-3) the diversity of the communities that comprise the Canadian cultural complex.

14 items to classify

Exercise 28-3 Appositive and Absolute Phrases

The appositive (Ap) and absolute (Ab) phrases in the following passage have been underlined. The word the appositives modify has been placed in bold print.

<u>Your ticket firmly grasped in your hand</u> **(Ab)**, you are off to an NHL hockey game. What can you expect from your experience in an era when there are almost five times as many teams as there were fifty years ago? Your local **team**, <u>the team that plays closest to where you live</u> **(Ap)**, will often have a large following if you live in Canada. For instance, the **Toronto Maple Leafs**, <u>the team of southern Ontario</u>, **(Ap)** have a fan base that is so large that it is almost impossible to get tickets to a game. It is not uncommon to hear stories about **long-time fans**, <u>ticket holders who inherited tickets that have been in the family for more than thirty years</u> **(Ap)**. These **fans**, <u>the ones who have been loyal to a team that has not won the</u>

Stanley Cup since 1967, **(Ap)** deserve better.

    Of course, the difficulty in purchasing tickets to games in some Canadian markets is compounded by ticket resellers. The face price for an inexpensive ticket may be $35, but the resale **price**, the price you will have to pay for a ticket that someone is reselling,**(Ap)** may be $100. I have even heard season ticket holders boast that they can sell some of their tickets, go to select games, and do so at no cost at all because of the profit they make from reselling the tickets. Thus, the **tickets** priced by the hockey team for families, the ones usually in the top of the arena, **(Ap)** no longer make for an inexpensive night out.

    Yet the story of the NHL fan does not end with the story of the long-time season ticket holder or the price of tickets. A close look at the individual fan tells another story. Her money paid out for tickets, **(Ab)** the keen hockey fan now has only to think about the cost of food, drink, and souvenirs, which have become a part of the game experience. A simple baseball **cap**, one with the team's logo on it, **(Ap)** can cost between $25 to $30, and this is one of the least expensive souvenirs. A game **jersey**, one with a player's name and number on it, **(Ap)** can cost over $300. Think how sad it can be. Her banner waving while proudly wearing her newly purchased player jersey, **(Ab)** the avid hockey fan approaches the stadium, ticket in hand, only to find out that her favourite player has been traded that morning for "future considerations."

11 phrases in total

Exercise 28-4 All Phrase Types

In the following passage the phrases have been underlined and marked as to whether they are participial (Part), gerundial (G), infinitive (I), appositive (Ap), absolute (Ab), or prepositional (P).

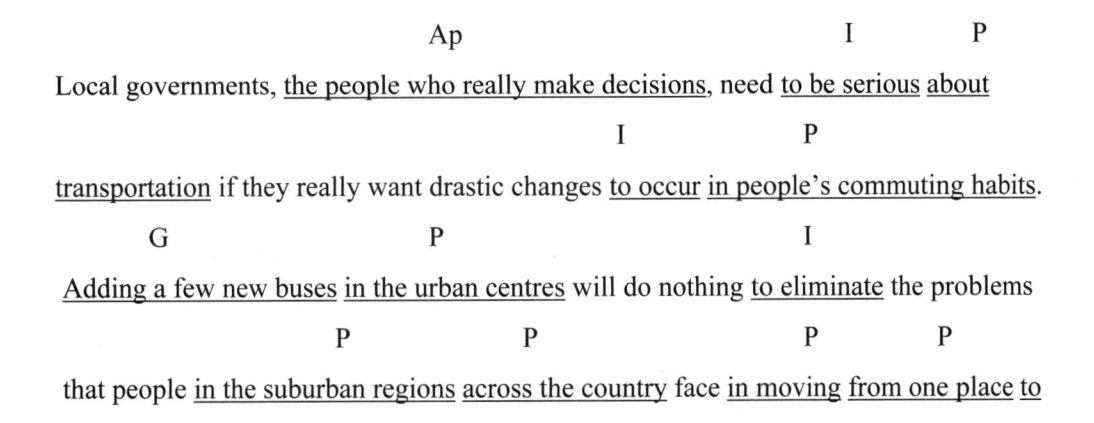

                            Ap   I   P
Local governments, the people who really make decisions, need to be serious about
                                     I   P
transportation if they really want drastic changes to occur in people's commuting habits.
    G   P   I
Adding a few new buses in the urban centres will do nothing to eliminate the problems
             P   P   P   P
that people in the suburban regions across the country face in moving from one place to

    P   I   I   P   G

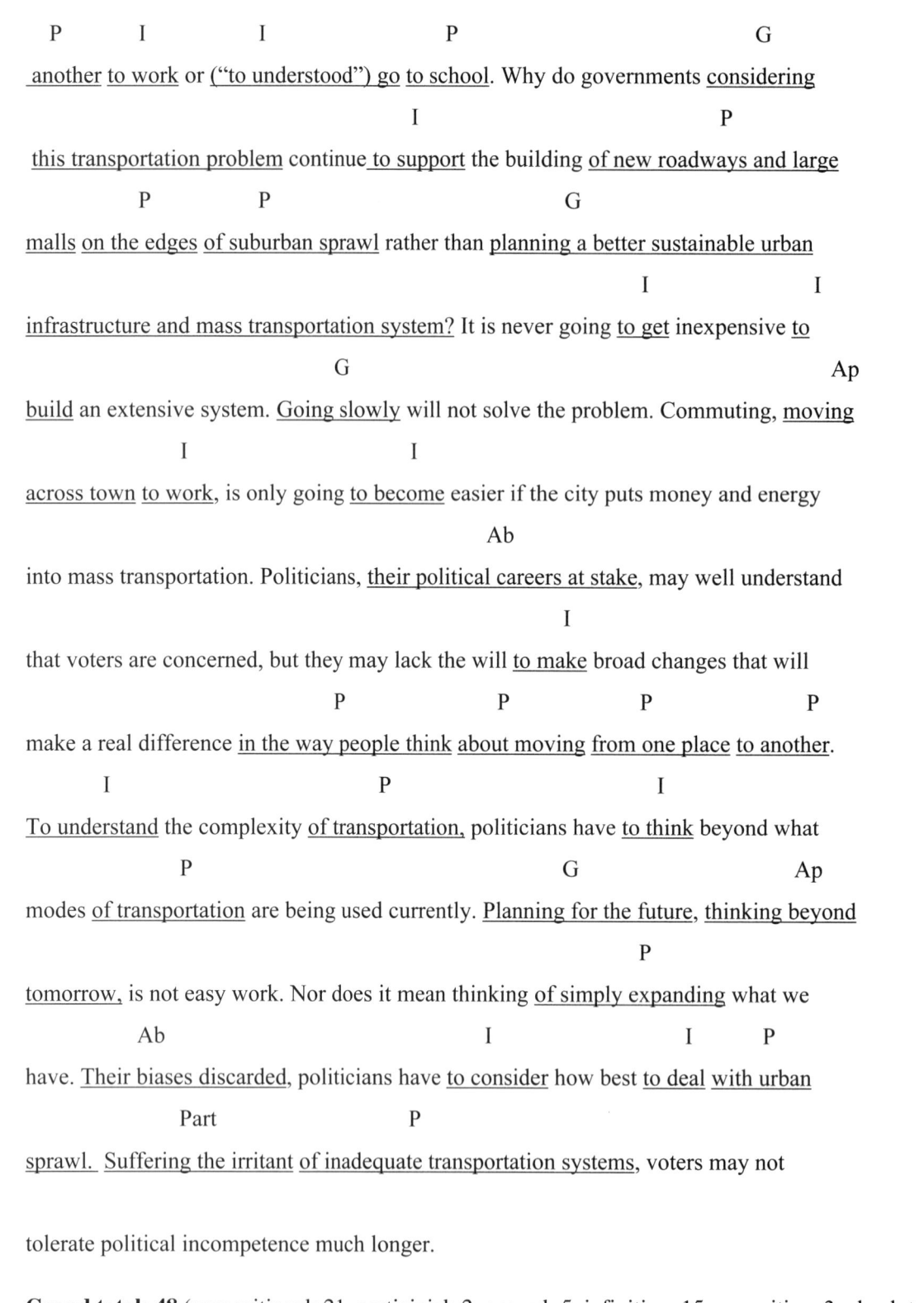

another to work or ("to understood") go to school. Why do governments considering

              I   P

this transportation problem continue to support the building of new roadways and large

   P   P   G

malls on the edges of suburban sprawl rather than planning a better sustainable urban

                      I   I

infrastructure and mass transportation system? It is never going to get inexpensive to

          G   Ap

build an extensive system. Going slowly will not solve the problem. Commuting, moving

    I   I

across town to work, is only going to become easier if the city puts money and energy

           Ab

into mass transportation. Politicians, their political careers at stake, may well understand

                  I

that voters are concerned, but they may lack the will to make broad changes that will

        P   P   P   P

make a real difference in the way people think about moving from one place to another.

 I   P   I

To understand the complexity of transportation, politicians have to think beyond what

    P   G   Ap

modes of transportation are being used currently. Planning for the future, thinking beyond

                  P

tomorrow, is not easy work. Nor does it mean thinking of simply expanding what we

  Ab   I   I P

have. Their biases discarded, politicians have to consider how best to deal with urban

   Part   P

sprawl. Suffering the irritant of inadequate transportation systems, voters may not

tolerate political incompetence much longer.

Grand total: 48 (prepositional: 21, participial: 2, gerund: 5, infinitive: 15, appositive: 3, absolute: 2)

Exercise 28-5 Constructing Phrases

The following answers for this exercise are not the only ones that could have been constructed to complete the sentences, but they should guide you in determining whether your answers are right.

1. Down [prepositional phrase] **in the rough** lay the golf ball.
2. I wanted [infinitive phrase] **to see** if I could strike the ball where it lay.
3. [participial phrase] **Looking at the ball**, I noticed that there was a rock right in front of it.
4. [Gerundial phrase] **Hitting the ball** onto the fairway was not going to be easy.
5. I was going [infinitive phrase] **to determine** if I could accomplish the task.
6. Gordon, [appositive phrase] **my golf buddy**, came over to see my plight.
7. [absolute phrase] **Looking amazed at my situation**, he suggested I take a penalty stroke and move the ball.
8. After all, he reasoned, a ball [restrictive appositive phrase] **dropped on the fairway** would be much easier to hit than what faced me in the rough.
9. [participial phrase] **Examining my situation**, I quickly saw he was right.
10. [gerundial phrase] **Being prudent** was the correct course of action. I picked up the ball and dropped it on the fairway where I could hit it without fear of having it bounce right back at me.

Exercise 28-6 Adding Phrases to Clauses

The suggested answers below are only examples. There a wide variety of answers that would be correct as long as they have the form of the type of phrase you have been asked to supply.

1. The 2008 financial crisis, [appositive phrase] **an unexpected collapse of major American financial institutions because of reckless loans**, generated pain for Americans first and for the rest of the world next.
2. Wall Street, [prepositional phrase] **in the first public judgment**, was seen as the culprit, but we quickly learned that the American government was also at fault.
3. The Canadian banking authorities began [infinitive phrase] **to feel vindicated** when it became clear that their restrictions on approving mortgages were prudent and necessary checks.
4. [absolute phrase] **Astonished by the depth and extent of the collapse**, the American public couldn't believe that financial experts could create a mess that wound up killing their own companies.

Answer Key   189

5. Canadian investors, [participial phrase] **annoyed at the emerging news**, soon discovered that all but one Canadian bank had heavy investments in American sub-prime mortgage funds.

6. [prepositional phrase] **After an embarrassing period**, however, our banks had the resources to overcome the losses caused by the sub-prime mortgage collapse.

7. [gerund phrase] **Being a reckless and greedy banker**, it appears, takes as much energy as being a prudent banker.

8. The bubble payment, [appositive phrase] **a part of the sub-prime mortgage structure**, was the first factor to cause people to walk away from their sub-prime mortgages and initiate the financial collapse of some major American financial institutions.

9. [absolute phrase] **His voice suppressing the anger of a Republican intervening in the marketplace**, President Bush was forced to appeal to Congress to approve a bailout of the American financial industry.

10. Ironically, [prepositional phrase] **for the second time in a generation**, the world was treated to the spectacle of the American government rescuing the financial industry from a collapse fuelled primarily by greed.

Exercise 28-7 Clauses

In the following passage the independent clauses (ICs) have been placed in bold print and the dependent clauses (DCs) have been underlined. The type of dependent clause, adverbial, adjectival, or noun, has been indicated above all the dependent clauses.

                  Adj clause   Noun clause

The problem <u>most students have composing an essay</u> **is** <u>they do not have a thesis</u>

        Adj clause   Adv clause

or major claim <u>that is well formed</u>. <u>Unless they learn to limit their focus</u>, **they will find**

                    Adv clause

their task very difficult. <u>When students start to write an essay</u>, **they can**

                    Adv clause

become overwhelmed by the task. <u>Unless they utilize prewriting strategies</u>, **they may**

even find it hard to develop a well-formed topic with a clear thesis. The best

beginning strategy is to write down all the points relative to the topic. Then, the

task becomes easier, for it is an easy step from a list of relevant points to using a

mind-map, free-writing, or applying the Pentad to focus their topic and isolate a
                    Adv clause

thesis. Once they have done that, **they can consider how to further organize their**
                        Adv clause

material. Although a formal outline is often the next step that students take in the writing
                    Noun clause direct object   Adj clause

process, they should first consider what points they have gathered that are most central

to their argument and to the length of their paper. **These are essentials factors to take**
                  Adv clause

into account. If students neglect to narrow their topic in this way, **they may find** they are
    Noun clause direct object   Adj clause

spending a considerable amount of time working on material they will eventually have to

cut.

Part VI SENTENCE ELEMENTS

Chapter 29 Parts of a Sentence

Exercise 29-1 Identifying Parts of Sentences—Subjects

In the answer key that follows, the complete subjects are underlined and the simple subjects are italicized.

1. In 2008, one female *leader* and four male *leaders* led their parties in the election to determine Canada's next government.

2. Most *commentators* agreed that, in the televised October debate among those leaders, the *head* of the Green Party was the most aggressive in advancing her ideas and attacking the ideas of her competitors.

3. In one of the debate's liveliest exchanges, *she* lectured Stephen Harper, the sitting prime minister, on his shortcomings.

4. Intriguingly, that same night, on American television, Senator *Joe Biden*, vice-presidential nominee of the Democratic Party, and Governor *Sarah Palin*, vice-presidential nominee of the Republican Party, debated their parties' respective positions.

5. In the newspapers the next day, the *survey* of audience response showed our preference for Biden and Palin over Dion, Duceppe, Harper, Layton, and May.

6. Though an unexpected result, <u>*we*</u> should recognize that <u>*our preferring*</u> the American debate over the Canadian debate is understandable.
7. <u>*Most* of us</u> were more focused on American candidates than on Canadian ones because of their novelty.
8. Why would <u>the average *Canadian*</u> be startled to learn of the novelty of Biden and Palin over people appearing on our television news repeatedly?
9. Isn't <u>*novelty*</u> the principal quality the Canadian viewer of television seeks?
10. Therefore, <u>*May, Biden,* and *Palin*</u> proved to be more interesting characters to Canadian viewers than Harper, Layton, Duceppe, and Dion.

Exercise 29-2 Identifying Parts of Sentences—Clauses

In the following exercise, the clause subjects have been placed in bold and the clause predicates have been underlined. As dependent clauses may be part of an independent clause and be embedded in it, all of the dependent clauses have been marked with "DC." In the following answer key, there are cases where the subject of a dependent clause is in the predicate of an independent clause and is both in bold type and underlined

1. <u>Over the past decade,</u> **newspaper columnists and television commentators** <u>have</u>
    DC
    <u>remarked</u> that **young adults** <u>have been voting less and less frequently</u> and that
        DC   DC
    <u>**those who**</u> <u>do vote</u> <u>are the children of parents</u> <u>**who**</u> <u>vote.</u>

2. <u>Recently,</u> **Rick Mercer,** <u>in his CBC program, pointed out</u> that, during elections,
    DC
    politicians <u>make sure they visit seniors' homes.</u> **Seniors** <u>always vote,</u> and **the**
                                                          DC
    politicians <u>pay attention to seniors' concerns</u> because **they** <u>vote.</u>
                                                                               DC

3. <u>On the other hand,</u> **he** <u>observed</u> that **politicians** <u>don't seem to be as concerned</u>
    <u>about attending all-candidates meetings on campuses across Canada</u> because
        DC
    young people <u>frequently don't exercise their right to vote.</u>

4. **He** <u>noted</u> that if **young people** <u>started voting en masse</u>, **politicians** <u>would make</u>
                   DC   DC

   <u>young Canadians' concerns a part of their political party's election platforms.</u>

5. **This** <u>proves the old adage</u> that **the squeaky wheel** <u>gets the grease</u>, and **the track**
                                                 DC

   record of politicians <u>is something young Canadians should pay attention to at</u>

   <u>election time</u>.

6. **Politicians** <u>are only concerned about</u> what **the people** **who** <u>do vote</u> <u>think</u>.
                                              DC   DC

7. If **you** <u>want to have an effect on</u> how **your government** <u>is acting</u>, **you** <u>have to</u>

   <u>be active and vote</u>.

8. If **you** <u>don't vote</u>, **you** <u>can only blame yourself</u> when **the government** <u>is not</u>
                       DC

   <u>doing</u> what **you** <u>want</u>.

9. <u>Next time</u> **you** <u>are tempted to say</u> **politicians** <u>are boring</u>, **[you understood]**
                       DC

   <u>remember</u> that **they** <u>do have an effect on your life</u>.

10. **They and the legislation they pass** <u>may affect your future</u>.

Exercise 29-3 Direct Objects, Indirect Objects, Subject Complements, and Object Complements

In the following exercise, the elements have been underlined and identified using the following key:

    Direct object = DO   *Indirect object = IO*
    Subject complement = SC *Object complement = OC*

Answer Key   193

1. When hockey season starts in the fall, every city and town across the country feels
     SC
   optimistic about its hockey club.

                                   DO
2. Newspaper writers watch the members of their team at training camp and write
   DO
   stories about how fresh and excited all the players look.

        SC
3. It is a time of optimism.

                                       DO
4. Neither fans nor reporters are assessing the team realistically.

5. When the puck drops in the first pre-season game, the columnists' attention
            SC
   becomes acute.

                         DO   IO   DO
6. The new players attack the puck and show the coaching staff their speed and skill.

                             SC
7. To some, the pre-season is the proving ground.

                                              DO   OC
8. At the end of the pre-season, the coaching staff cut players not performing at the NHL level.

                      SC   SC
9. The players know the coach's decisions are important.

                                   DO   OC
10. Not surprisingly, the coaches make the players with potential their priority.

Chapter 30 Sentence Patterns

Exercise 30-1 Identifying Sentence Patterns

In the following exercise the sentence pattern of each sentence have been identified using the following key:

   1. Subject–verb
   2. Subject–verb–subject complement
   3. Subject–verb–direct object
   4. subject–verb–indirect object–direct object
   5. subject–verb–direct object–object complement

   1. Today, job opportunities are changing quickly. [1]

   2. It is hard for students to find a career path. [2]

   3. People starting off in a career want an interesting, secure job. [3]

   4. Yet gone are the days of the one-job career. [2]

194   Answer Key

5. A secure career is a challenge to find. [2]
6. Students must examine each potential career carefully. [3]
7. Careers change. [1]
8. Advisers must tell students the truth. [4]
9. Students must be vigilant. [2]
10. They do not see their education as an unmitigated disaster or a waste of time and money. [5]
11. Their parents may have loaned them money to enable them to complete their education. [4]
12. The axiom "education for an education's sake" is not appropriate anymore. [2]
13. To get an education, many students incur a large debt. [3]
14. The country needs a well-educated youth to ensure its future welfare. [3]
15. Governments should supply students an opportunity to acquire a career. [4]
16. But that career should give them the opportunity to earn a living as well as benefit their country. [4]
17. In elections, ["you" understood] vote for those who support these values. [1]

Chapter 31 Identifying Sentence Types

Exercise 31-1

In the following passage the sentences have been identified using the following symbols: a simple sentence (S), a compound sentence (C), a complex sentence (Cx) or a compound-complex sentence (CC)

[Cx] What is it most students look for in a postsecondary institution? [Cx] Every year, *Maclean's* magazine publishes an issue that lists the "best schools" in Canada, a list that ranks institutions from coast to coast. [Cx] The magazine advertises that its survey will help students find the universities that have the best students, the best professors, the best food, and the best loans and scholarships. [CC] Yet is the survey that *Maclean's* has published annually since 1990 of much use, and do students actually use it? [Cx] When examining the survey, readers need to ask how comprehensive a survey it is when it does not include reviews of a large number of postsecondary institutions in Canada.

[Cx] When many students make the decision to follow a postsecondary course of studies, they consider a number of elements. [CC] They consider how close to home the institution is, and they consider what programs the institution offers. [S] They will, of course, take their peers' opinions into consideration when making their decision. [S] These considerations may be tempered by a number of other factors. [S] The cost of the education may be of paramount concern to the student. [Cx] If the student has good grades in high school and can win a scholarship, tuition fees may not be as strong a concern as they would be for a student who does not have a high GPA.

[Cx] One of the factors related to students' postsecondary studies is tied to whether or not they are taking a full course load or studying part-time. [S] This fact alone is worthy of study. [S] Why would a student want to prolong his or her studies for a degree from four years to eight? [CC] A quick survey might reveal that students often cannot afford to go to college or university full-time because of finances; it might also reveal that a large percentage of students are working part-time at low-paying jobs to make their studies possible. [CC] To add to their troubles, students who arrive on campuses across Canada for the first time are not always sure what course of studies they want to follow, and they are not necessarily aware of their own strengths and weaknesses. [Cx] A large number of students who want to be doctors are unaware of the qualities and educational abilities they must possess to be a successful medical school candidate.

[Cx] Students often do not know what they want to do with their education. [Cx] They do know that the type of service job they will get with only a high school education will pay poorly. [Cx] Whether or not they consider the numerous opportunities that postsecondary education has to offer them is an interesting question. [Cx] If they were to read the *Maclean's* review, they might ignore fields of study where they could be happy and gainfully employed. [Cx] There are careers in the trades and technologies that are interesting and lucrative. [CC] *Maclean's* falls short of its duty to publish information that is helpful for all Canadians looking for an education, and it falls short in ways that could easily be rectified if the magazine took a more comprehensive view of education. [Cx] If it did take these limitations into consideration, it might create an analysis that was meaningful to a broader range of Canadians. [C] That would benefit young Canadians, and it would also benefit *Maclean's*.

Chapter 33 Sentence Variety

Exercise 33-1 Editing Sentences for Variety

The following example should not be considered definitive. It illustrates one way of reducing an excess of simple sentences into a paragraph with sufficient variety in its sentences. Compare it with your own version and see if you have introduced enough sentence variety.

One interesting element in the cost of gas is the profit level of gas stations. Despite reports of the largest profits ever earned in the history of capitalism being declared by Exxon—eleven billion dollars in the first quarter of 2008, fourteen billion dollars in the third quarter—gas stations do not enjoy the same profit margins as oil companies. Even stations carrying the names of Shell and Petro-Canada earn modest profits. We know that independent gas stations are struggling because the Canadian Independent Petroleum Marketers Association has pointed out that these stations average four to six cents per litre in profit and have to pay as much as two cents per litre per transaction of that profit to the credit card companies whose cards they honour. These stations have to buy their gas on the open market and are forced to match the prices charged by other stations, including those franchised by oil companies. Additionally, the rapid escalation in oil and gas prices has forced people to drive less. The twin problems of very small profit margins coupled with a nation-wide decline in the number of miles driven by people have been hard on the independent gas station. Even a change in the price of oil is unlikely to return prosperity to these stations. We cannot be happy about that.

9 sentences in length

Data from Aleksandar Zivojinovic. "Why the Real 'Corner Gas' Is in Trouble," *Maclean's,* July 28, 2008, p. 39.

Exercise 33-2 Editing Sentences for Variety

The following example should not be considered definitive. It illustrates one way of reducing an excess of simple sentences into a paragraph with sufficient variety in its sentences. Compare it with your own version and see if you have introduced enough sentence variety.

In the fall of 2008, a far-reaching financial collapse upset the stock markets of the United States, Europe, Australia, New Zealand, Hong Kong, and Japan. Within a single week, the American stock market lost 18 per cent of its value, the European markets declined by 22 percent, and Japan's market declined by 24 percent. The astonishing facet of this widespread retrenchment in value was that it began with American house owners walking away from their houses and precipitating a collapse in real estate values. Between 2002 and 2005, Americans had bought new homes in unprecedented numbers, driven in large part by financial agencies approving mortgages for people who did not qualify for them in any traditional way. The third year catch-up payment written into these mortgages and the unreasonably low level of monthly payments set up the holders of the mortgages for failure when they had to make a large single payment and realistic monthly payments. Granting mortgages to unqualified borrowers heated up the housing market and allowed the lenders to bundle mortgages into financial packages eagerly purchased by other financial agencies. The house of cards collapsed as soon as the holders of the mortgages stopped paying for them and walked away. Foreclosures didn't help because there were no replacement buyers, and the net result was a decline in housing values. The worthless mortgages held by financial companies meant they couldn't pay their debts, and many simply failed and declared bankruptcy. Inevitably the values in the stock market declined sharply because of this failure of companies driven by greed and foolish practices.

10 sentences in length

Part VIII GRAMMATICAL SENTENCES

Chapter 41 Construction

Exercise 41-1

In each of the following questions, the answer is given in the dotted lines; in most cases, there is no single right answer.

1. One interesting dimension of the financial recession that started in 2008 was the decline of an American car industry they faced bankruptcy by the end of the year.
   FUSED The easiest correction here is to place a semicolon between "industry" and "they. You could also place a period after "industry" or use a conjunction in place of the semicolon or period.

2. Despite the fact that GM was the largest company in the world less than ten years ago, it is now facing bankruptcy.
   CORRECT No correction is necessary; the sentence is correct.

3. Ford is thinking of selling its majority share of Volvo stock, the company believes it will need the money that generates to avoid bankruptcy in the first half of 2009.
   COMMA SPLICE You can fix this by inserting a semicolon between" stock" and "they." Alternatively, you might insert a conjunction such as "since" or 'because" after "stock."

4. Not long ago, Chrysler was in serious talks with GM to determine if GM could take over the Chrysler company, alternatively, it wanted to explore with GM the possibility of becoming a junior partner.
   COMMA SPLICE Try fixing this error by placing a period after "company." Remember to capitalize "alternatively."

5. During 2008, Toyota became the largest seller of cars and trucks in the United States, displacing GM from its traditional occupancy of that position.
   CORRECT No change is needed.

6. Perhaps no other statistic is so telling as the actual price of a share of General Motors stock by the latter months of 2008, that share had fallen to a rate equalling its value in 1950.
   FUSED A new independent clause starts after "stock." You can insert a period or a semicolon there and start a new clause.

7. Observers look for simple reasons to explain the decline in the value and solvency of large American car manufacturers, the chief reason is that they ceased making what North Americans wanted.

   COMMA SPLICE Probably the simplest fix here is to insert a period in place of the comma following "manufacturers" and capitalizing "the." You could also use a semicolon or a conjunction in place of the comma

8. That reason alone, however, would not have led to the virtual collapse of the largest business in America; there had to be other contributing causes.

   CORRECT The semicolon is an appropriate substitute for a conjunction.

9. Perhaps the most important of those subsidiary causes was the fact that it cost American carmakers more to make a car their competitors could build a plant in America and produce cars more cheaply.

   FUSED The run-on sentence starts after the word "car." You could insert a period or a semicolon here.

10. Ironically, one of the key reasons American carmakers lost the battle for market supremacy was a very simple fact their traditional customers turned to foreign imports.

    FUSED The run-on sentence starts after the word "fact." Insert a period or colon here or restructure the two clauses so that one of them is dependent.

Exercise 41-2 Recognizing Fragments

In the following answer key the corrections are added in brackets. At times, the statement may have been joined to a sentence preceding it or following it. If the original sentence was correct, it is followed by a [C]. You may come up with different corrections for the sentences.

1. As more and more Canadians live in urban centres, it is easy to forget that, at the beginning of the last century, most of Canada's population lived in small towns or in the countryside. [C]
2. Sadly enough[, w]e have become less and less aware of our rural heritage.
3. Yet small communities still have an impact on the way we see the country and what we value as Canadians. [C]
4. Driving through the countryside, [we really see] Canada.
5. [We see the] small villages in photographs, the vistas of what seem to be endless prairies.
6. Those are defining images that we see again and again in photographic essays on the country.
7. [We also see images of moose] in lakes, and prairie dogs beside the road on hind legs.

8. Images like these typify Canada[,]
9. [as] do, in contrast, pictures of Vancouver and Victoria's historic Chinatowns.
10. However, we are just as likely to identify with the image of the rolling Alberta foothills with cattle spread out across them as we are to an image of a cowboy at the Calgary stampede. [C]
11. But do Canadians recognize images of the Williams Lake Rodeo [and]
12. [joined to sentence 11] Peggy's Cove?
13. [Are they familiar with photographs of] the mouth of the Saguenay River?
14. Even though we may not recognize photographs of all of these places, we [are] proud of our land[,]
15. [a]nd recognize that it has a varied landscape and people.
16. Images [ ] define who we are as much as where we live.
17. Urban images and ones of people, too [, explain who we are].
18. St. John's, Halifax, Montreal, Toronto, Winnipeg, Calgary, Edmonton, and Vancouver [may be a part of the recognizable Canadian landscape,]
19. [b]ut we should not forget that we are a nation of diverse peoples and places. [C]
20. [We are v]ery diverse indeed.

Exercise 41-3 Correcting Fragments

The first version below identifies the errors in sentence construction in the original paragraph. Following that, you will find a revised and corrected version of the paragraph. Your rewritten version may be different, but it must correct the errors in sentence construction noted here.

It is startling to read that General Motors might disappear into bankruptcy before the end of 2009 **FUSED** this was, not long ago, the largest company in the world. What a shock **FRAGMENT**. Among a host of reasons for the swift fall of GM are two central reasons. The first is the fact it has been unionized longer than any other car company, **COMMA SPLICE** the second is their attachment to large vehicles The agreements that GM signed with unions as long as fifty years ago **FRAGMENT**. The company Presidents and board members never foresaw that agreeing to pension plans would mean that the most expensive component in a Cadillac **FRAGMENT**. It would be the $1,500 per auto coming out of a GM plant it takes to pay for the medical and pension benefits of retired workers. Compare that amount to the $300 per auto Toyota pays for the same benefit. While also producing cars and trucks in the United States **FRAGMENT**. But it was not only the failure of GM to prepare for the expenditures necessary to comply with the collective agreements it signed with its unions that placed it in jeopardy.

While European and Asian manufacturers perfected compact vehicles powered by efficient four-cylinder motors **FRAGMENT**. GM persisted in sending large number of vehicles to its showrooms that were built on a truck platform. Most frequently with a six- or eight-cylinder engine inside it **FRAGMENT**. When times were good, consumers accepted the costs associated with gassing up and running such large vehicles, whether trucks or SUVs. But the combination of a brief but intense inflation of oil prices and a sudden deflation of the American economy **FRAGMENT**. And other economies for that matter **FRAGMENT**. GM was not ready for the collapse of its traditional market **FUSED** they had not anticipated the sudden decline of customers interested in large vehicles. Or in any vehicles at all **FRAGMENT**. The Silverado truck was once a proud American icon. Having become a symbol of a manufacturer unable to perceive where the market was heading **FRAGMENT**. Although the federal government has come to the aid of the three large American carmakers, their future remains uncertain, **COMMA SPLICE** we do not know if there will be one, two, or three American carmakers by the end of 2009. Or none **FRAGMENT**.

NOTE: In the following sample rewrite of the paragraph, the underlined/italicized parts show where changes were made to the original.

It is *shocking* to read that General Motors might disappear into bankruptcy before the end of 2009 because this was, not long ago, the largest company in the world. Among a host of reasons for the swift fall of GM are two central reasons. The first is the fact it has been unionized longer than any other car company, *and the second* is its attachment to large vehicles. The agreements that GM signed with unions as long as fifty years ago included pension plans and health benefits *at a cost that presidents and boards of the company never adequately anticipated, a cost that today constitutes the most expensive component in a Cadillac*. At $1,500 per auto, *this cost is five times greater than the $300* paid by Toyota for the same benefit enjoyed by its American workers. But it was not only the failure of GM to prepare for the expenditures necessary to comply with the collective agreements it signed with its unions that placed it in jeopardy. While European and Asian manufacturers perfected compact vehicles powered by efficient four-cylinder *engines, GM persisted* in sending large numbers of vehicles to its showrooms that were built on truck platforms and equipped with six- and even eight-cylinder engines. When times were good, consumers accepted the costs associated with gassing up and running such large vehicles, whether trucks or SUVs. But the combination of a brief but intense inflation of oil prices and a sudden deflation of the American economy *and other economies, proved lethal*. GM was not ready for the collapse of its traditional *market; it had not* foreseen the sudden decline of customers interested in large, expensive vehicles *or customers who decided they could make do with the vehicle they were driving.* The Silverado truck, once a proud American icon, *became a symbol* of a manufacturer unable to comprehend where the market was heading. Although the federal government has come to the aid of the three large American carmakers, their future remains *uncertain. We* do not know if there will be one, two, or three carmakers in the near future. *There may even be none.*

Chapter 42 Agreement

Exercise 42-1 Subject-Verb Agreement

The corrections in subject–verb agreement have been underlined and highlighted in bold type in the passage below.

One of the financial analysts I read recently **has dedicated** his column to how the markets are manipulated. Neither the individual investor nor the large stockholders **are** aware of the forces that affect the value of their investments on a day-to-day basis. The large shareholders, as well as the small investor, **are** often unaware of the real reasons why investment prices fluctuate. Individual stocks **and** even the bond market **rise** and **fall** in ways that perplex analysts. The young investor and the old investor alike **are** told to hold on to an investment and to depend on its long-term appreciation. This and other sage advice **is** of little comfort when investors want access to the money tied up in their investment. An investment team that **is** studying the market to counsel its clients may have to reconsider its strategy. Every **investment counsellor wants** to retain his or her clients; without clients, **he or she** would be out of work. Thus, some of the counsellors' advice **is** geared to maintaining the investment activity of clients. There **are** some counsellors, though, who may temper their advice, realizing that they have to protect their clients in the short term and wait for better returns and more commissions in the future. That, however, may not put food on their plates or money in their wallets in the short run. The problems of the counsellors **are** of little comfort to investors, who **see** their investments below cost. How can investors feel comfortable knowing the market is manipulated in ways that they cannot foresee or fathom?

16 errors

Exercise 42-2 Verb Tense and Mood Agreement

1. **TENSE** In 2007, Canadians **were** going south of their border to buy cars at reduced prices.
2. One year later, they were not importing cars from the States; in fact, they were not buying as many Canadian cars either. **CORRECT**

3. **MOOD** This change was a result of the collapsing economy. If GM **were** in charge of that economy, the cars would still be selling, and we would have more disposable income.
4. **TENSE** When the leaders of the American carmakers appeared in Washington before the Senate inquiry committee, they **were** foolish enough to be televised stepping off private jets. Later, they wondered why senators criticized this choice of transportation.
5. **TENSE** One month later, when the same leaders appeared again to argue their need for government support, they **were** driving hybrids. Interestingly, at least one of those hybrids **was** an SUV, demonstrating that they never fully understood the first criticism.
6. **TENSE** In the end, both the American and Canadian governments **decided** that support for the North American car industry **was** necessary. Many citizens in both countries felt the companies should be left to deal with their own mess.
7. **MOOD** If it **were** you making the decision, what would you do?
8. **TENSE** In some ways, a company like GM, which **drove** its stock value down from twenty-nine dollars a share in 2000 to two dollars and forty cents in 2008, deserved to be left to find its own way out.
9. **TENSE** But the politicians **realized** that there were an extremely large number of citizens who would be hurt by the failure of even one of the big three companies. For instance, the average salary of an auto assembly plant worker **was** nearly thirty-two dollars an hour.
10. **MOOD** Even a worker at a plant manufacturing auto parts averages twenty-four dollars an hour. If the auto maker **were** to fail and go into bankruptcy, tens of thousands of workers would turn overnight from citizens paying mortgages, taxes, and living expenses into unemployed people eligible for unemployment pay.
11. **TENSE** It was the sheer size of the automobile industry that **intimidated** elected representatives, driving them to vote money for support of the companies rather than following their instincts and leaving the private sector alone.
12. **TENSE** Not surprisingly, many elected representatives of right-wing parties followed their ideological values and **refused** to vote support.
13. Again, if it had been you making this decision, what would you have done? **CORRECT**
14. **TENSE** The great fear of all those who **supported** the rescue of these companies must have been the possibility that the rescue would not work in the end. Both GM and Chrysler desperately offered price reductions on their product and completed plans to lay off many more workers in light of the decreased demand in North America for new vehicles.

15. **MOOD** Ironically, if this reduction in demand **were** happening in 2010, GM would have the Volt, their new electric car, and a number of hybrids to offer in response to the public's demand for autos offering low gas consumption.

Exercise 42-3 Pronoun–Antecedent Agreement

In the following passage, the errors in pronoun-antecedent agreement have been underlined and corrected.

How many sets of wires connect your television, DVD, CD player, speakers, and tuner? For most folks, the area where all these items converge is spaghetti central. Ironically, the tangle of wires is just the overt symptom of the many small nagging puzzles that can arise when you connect a number of audio-video devices to one another. Even if you have only a DVD, a television, and speakers, you can be guaranteed **their wiring** will give you problems. Add on a high-definition device like a PVR, a CD player, and a tuner, and suddenly complications arise. Neither the devices nor **their** wiring is simple or can be set up quickly. Each device has to be properly hooked up to the correct input sockets on the tuner for **it** to run correctly. Neither the CD player nor the DVD player will run on the same circuit as each has **its** own sound amplification needs. Even when you have successfully configured your system, operating malfunctions will still occur when you least expect **them**. One of the components loses **its** connections. Suddenly, there is no sound. You slide your components out to see what the problem is. Each of the wires has wrapped **itself** around other wires, and you can't see clearly what connects to what. The wires all look the same. In addition, **they are** all tangled up with the other wires. It is not enough to find the one wire that appears to have a bad connection at one end; you have to trace **it** to the other end to make sure you have the right wire. Each wire and connection has to be checked to make sure **it is** secure.

10 errors

Exercise 42-4 Pronoun Reference Problems

1. Since anyone can attend the film showing tonight, it is hard to check **him or her** at the door.
2. Either the one-sided games or the increase in ticket prices **is** the reason for the decline in attendance at football games.
3. **CORRECT**
4. Her sisters **are** not ready for the family holiday that starts next week, and neither **is** she.

5. The committee announced **its** recommendations after completing the investigation that occupied four months.

6. There **are** a number of reasons why you will not pass your statistics course this semester.

7. **CORRECT**

8. The Canadian bomb disposal division will have **its** first scheduled break from duty next month.

9. Every person has to ensure that **he or she** has signed the proper forms before taking an approved holiday.

10. Many of the Americans who voted for a President in 2008 were casting **their vote** for the first time in **their** **life**.

Exercise 42-5 Unclear Pronoun Reference

One of the problems that **is** facing Asian food markets in 2009 is the shortfall in rice. Earthquakes, flooding, and interrupted growing seasons are a major part of the problem, but **these extraordinary events** have been compounded by wastage of what rice crops have been harvested. Spills, contamination by water, rats, and rot consume an estimated 15 percent of the harvested rice before it gets to the marketplace. Given that rice is a staple food throughout the region, **this wastage needs** to be addressed. The vermin and spillage problem interact because the holes eaten in sacks of rice let the rice fall out and decay on the floor. There **are** subsequent losses of product because of this simple problem. Many of the sacks holding the harvested rice have been crudely patched because of the high cost of new sacks, and this contributes to the level of lost product. Another of the many reasons causing the harvested grain to decline before getting to market **is** the leaking of barn and warehouse roofs. Once water has soaked the rice, it is no longer edible. The rot is often a result of the methods used to dry the harvested rice. Laid out on roads and other flat areas to dry, rice often stays there too long. It may be run over by vehicles, corrupted by oil and other substances, or eaten by birds, **thus decreasing** the size of the crop brought to market. The United Nations and individual countries have combined **their** forces to try and counter wastage. They know that the rice lost after harvesting and before marketing **is** sufficient to feed 184,000,000 people. A typical rice farm is small and its owner has little money. So buying poison to combat rats and mice, paying for new barn roofs, building special drying areas, and waterproofing trucks are beyond **the individual farmer** as strategies to fight waste. Everybody has to do **his or her** part in addressing this, however, especially now that famine faces many of these areas.

Chapter 43 Common Sentence Problems

Exercise 43-1 Misplaced Modifiers

In the following answer key, the misplaced modifiers have been moved next to the words they modify. The corrections are indicated.

In the past, politicians have said they would try and develop programs that are green, programs that will deal with the problem of global warming and the approaching shortage of petroleum products. **In a modern society**, much of society's development stems from items that are derived from oil. In *The Graduate,* **a popular 1960s movie**, one of the throwaway lines addressed to Dustin Hoffman, the main character, was that there was a great future in plastics. Indeed, you don't have to look very far to find out how plastics have become **almost** an integral element of our day-to-day lives. As I write this, my fingers are typing out the letters of each of the words on a plastic keyboard embedded in a plastic case. If you are holding a pen in your hand as you read this, it is likely made **almost** entirely of plastic. Ironically, when *The Graduate* was first released, most people laughed at the advice given to the new university graduate. We may not laugh so hard once we realize what our dependence on plastic means, especially as petroleum products that plastic are made out of are going to be in decline in the near future. **Only** time will tell if we adapt to rising oil prices and the effect that will have on so many products we are accustomed to using.

    The effect of petroleum products on the environment, however, is manifest in many ways. If we went shopping **thirty years ago**, we most likely had our purchase packed in a paper bag. Suddenly, most of the packaging industry shifted to **only** producing plastic bags. Now, everywhere we go, we find our purchases placed in plastic bags unless we make a point of bringing along our own cloth bags. The number of plastic bags **in garbage dumps** has developed into a major problem. Not only do these plastic bags not biodegrade, but they also blow out of the garbage dump and into the nearby countryside. Sometimes, they **even** get into the water system and end up in the ocean where they play havoc with seabirds and fish.

10 errors

Exercise 43-2 Dangling Modifiers

In the following passage, the errors have been crossed out and corrections are in bold type.

At the turn of the twenty-first century, the automobile industry in North America was looking at bigger and bigger cars, vans, and four-wheel drive SUVs that were not economical or fuel-efficient. ~~Looking back in time,~~ **If we examine the past, we will see that** cars had already been through one period in the

206   Answer Key

early 1980s when the price of fuel increased rapidly and the car-buying public changed its priorities. The same change in consumer behaviour occurred in 2008, but whether or not manufacturers or car owners would heed the shift was uncertain. ~~After almost a century of being seen as an essential symbol of success~~* **For a century, car owners had seen cars as symbols of success**, and they continued to take the advice of the auto industry and buy inefficient vehicles.

In 2008, something did happen that made people's heads turn. For the first time ever, the company that sold the most cars in the world was no longer a North American company. General Motors lost its mantle as the world's largest car manufacturer to Toyota, which outsold GM. ~~Seeing fuel efficiency as something that affected their pocketbooks,~~ **Car buyers became more attracted to** efficient, well-built cars than they had been before. Suddenly, the North American big three automakers were faced with a horrendous downturn in sales and unprecedented losses. ~~Thinking of how to maintain their corporations~~ [The corporations looked to Washington and Ottawa as good sources of assistance]. After all, the big three reasoned, as their CEOs got into their private jets, if we don't get aid, the number of people we will have to lay off will be politically unacceptable. ~~Getting into their jets the money already seemed a certainty~~* **As the CEOs got into their jets, they thought the money was a certainty**. **If they thought about** ~~Thinking about~~ the issue, **they could justify** the money ~~could be justified~~*. Caught up in their own delusion, **the CEOs could hear** the assembly lines ~~hummed~~ **humming** as they had in the past. Yet, as the auto industry was a mature industry, politicians reasoned that money should not be doled out without some strings attached, and they rejected the CEOs' proposals. Shamed and shunned, the CEOs of the big three returned to their corporations empty-handed. ~~Discouraged by their reception,~~ **The CEOs realized that** rethinking their strategy was as essential to their immediate survival as rethinking the line of automobiles they would roll off their assembly lines.

*Note: passive voice creates a dangling modifier here. Errors like this are more difficult to correct as you will have to change the sentence into active voice from passive voice in eliminating the dangling modifier.

9 errors

Exercise 43-3 Misplaced and Dangling Modifiers

The misplaced and dangling modifiers have been struck out, and the type of error (MM or DM) has been indicated next to the correction for each error, which appears in bold. You may come up with different answers from those in the answer key.

Answer Key   207

According to studies done recently, ~~by 2024,~~ peak oil production will occur **by 2024** **(MM)**. That means that, by 2024, the world will be producing the maximum oil flow it can expect from its known petroleum resources. ~~Looking beyond that date~~ **If we project beyond that date** **(DM)**, oil production will decrease, leaving the world with less oil and higher demand. If we think the past increase in the price of oil was an anomaly, we are mistaken. If demand continues to rise and oil consumption continues to increase, the world is headed for a major crisis. ~~Going down~~ **If we go down** **(DM)** the road we are on even five years without coming to terms with the technological shift that is urgently needed, oil will be in short supply and its price will start to spike again. This time, however, prices will not go down quickly. The world either has to come to terms with using less oil or find alternatives for it. The short period of time **in which we have become accustomed to inexpensive oil and gas** **(MM)** is coming to an end ~~in which we have become accustomed to inexpensive oil and gas~~. Ironically, building ~~exactly~~ more roads for more cars may be **exactly** **(MM)** the wrong thing to do at this juncture. Putting money into research on technologies that might help us cope with the dramatic shift that oil's shortage will necessitate might be a smarter alternative. ~~Now~~ Building mass transit **now** **(MM)** rather than encouraging more people to use their cars will help the situation, but building larger houses and more suburban communities will not help.

Besides the problem of peak oil production being only a few years away, according to a January 17, 2009, article in the *Vancouver Sun*, "25 per cent of the world's reserves are overstated" (C2). If that is true, the peak production of oil may be **even** **(MM)** closer than ~~even~~ experts think, and alternatives will be hard to implement soon enough to make a difference. Problems lie ahead in the immediate future. Given that we are worried about global warming, can we afford to switch our heating technology and electricity-generating technology back to coal? How will we cope with the rising cost of plastics and the many other by-products of petroleum? Similarly, the container, food storage, and general merchandise packaging manufacturers have components tied to oil. The shift away from oil or the increase in cost of oil-related goods will dramatically affect such industries. Finally, how do we rationalize the fact that, if post-industrial nations encourage energy conservation, the countries most affected will be emerging nations, where industrial growth and increased energy consumption are ~~almost~~ analogous to the growth of **almost** their whole economies?

~~Not paying close attention to this problem, a new Dark Age may be launched~~ **If we do not pay close attention to this problem,** **(DM and moving passive voice into active voice) we may be launching a new Dark Age**. It will be one caused not by cultural and religious intolerance but by a similar set of ignoble stances related to the consumption of energy. Whereas the Dark Age in Europe after the fall of the Roman Empire was figurative, the next Dark Age the world experiences may well be literal, as the lights and machines are switched off and we descend into a different type of human abyss. **Looking ahead, we still do not know** **(DM)** how such a downturn in human activity will affect societies around the world ~~remains to be seen~~. A profound downturn does suggest, though, that our current lifestyle will have to change. What all this means for political stability is anyone's guess.

4 dangling modifiers

6 misplaced modifiers

Exercise 43-4 Working with Parallel Structure

The following answer key either places CORRECT following the sentence or makes the necessary change or changes to avoid any faulty use of parallel structure. The changes are highlighted.

1. One of the new phenomena in the lives of the affluent is the presence in their homes of nannies, whose responsibilities include cleaning the house, getting the children to school, cooking meals, and **doing** laundry as required.
2. In the United States, nannies sometimes become a political issue when elected people hire someone who does not possess a green card, a formal record of entry to America, **or fluency in American English**.
3. Although it is not part of the nanny issue, Americans have expressed resentment about the number of illegal immigrants in their country, people working at jobs without holding green cards, without being formally registered, living in what amount to separate communities, and **avoiding** military service.
4. I was struck by the brevity of the message posted by the apartment building's laundry room by the caretaker. It read: a) use your own soap; b) take dry clothes **with you when you leave**; c) don't leave your laundry alone; d) lock the door **after using the laundry room.**
5. Most post-secondary institutions now have learning centres that attempt to help students to master the courses they are taking, **to** write papers in those courses, to learn proper study techniques, and to learn how to prepare for time-limited tests.
6. The simple fact that about 30 percent of post-secondary students disappear between the first and third years of study suggests that either more care and funding need to be invested in these study centres or **that entrance requirements should be changed**.
7. Considering that, across Canada, the Grade Twelve cohort has shrunk in recent years, post-secondary institutions are spending more energy on recruitment than on student success; more money on residences than on counselling; more time searching for cheaper, less experienced faculty than on creating buddy systems or learning groups; and more time getting students to enroll with them than on ensuring those students can be successful. **CORRECT**

8. One of the major areas where students struggle is in completing papers on time. A student enrolled in a full load of courses in Humanities will probably be required to write ten or more papers in a fourteen-week semester, and that means starting research a month ahead of the paper's due date, **drafting** a first effort early, and getting help from an instructor or a learning centre with that draft.

9. Students don't fail because of ability. It is more likely that a drop-out is caused by a lack of motivation, **a need to party every weekend because he or she is away from home**, an inability to plan a schedule that includes study and writing time, and a simple realization that it is too late to catch up once you have fallen behind.

10. Sadly, however, the disappearance of students after they have enrolled in a post-secondary institution robs Canada of educated workers, places youths at risk because of an inadequate preparation for the workplace, and puts too many people on paths to unemployment. **CORRECT**

Part IX USAGE AND DICTION

Chapter 44 Diction (Word Choice)

Exercise 44-1 Redundancy and Wordiness

In the following answer key, the errors are crossed out; suggestions for eliminating them are in bold. You may have handled the errors differently.

When we learned the law of gravity that stated **whatever goes up must come down**, we did not understand that it also applied to other aspects of life ~~beyond the laws of gravity that also go up and down~~ [redundant]. For instance, during the period between 1995 and 2007, everyone who was interested in investments thought that prices ~~were going in one direction only, that they~~ [redundant] **couldn't go anywhere but up**. House prices climbed every year, and those who were new to the real estate market accepted realtors' assurances that today's prices were a bargain, for the people marketing the new developments were sure to boost the prices ~~soon again~~ [wordy and unnecessary] as demand was higher than supply ~~and when that happened the price would increase, it would keep going higher and higher~~ [wordy and redundant]. Listening to that assertion, some even thought that buying and flipping new condos was a good way to turn a fast profit~~; in a short period of time, they reasoned, they could earn a vast amount of money reselling their investment~~ [redundant]. For a down payment of five percent of the asking price, they could reap the reward of reselling the condo for a five percent increase in the selling price ~~making for a big return on their small investment~~ [redundant], **a profit they could not obtain investing the same money** ~~in a savings account or other conservative investment~~ **conservatively**.

[wordy]. They did not factor in some of the other costs of such an investment—land transfer fees, real estate agent fees, or GST—which would eat into their profit margin. They had heard too many stories about **people who had done well in real estate.** ~~people who had made more money in real estate than in any other kind of investment~~ [redundant]. There were even investment seminars some of them had attended that had promised them windfall profits through buying and flipping houses and condos, ~~they too could make a fortune in a short period of time~~ [redundant].

During this time, even real estate agents got caught up in the euphoria of buying and selling houses. These agents actively looked for older houses they could buy, cosmetically renovate with a quick paint job, and flip for a comfortable profit. This practice also had an inflationary effect on the market. Suddenly, the best bargains were only on the market for days. People ~~competed with one another and~~ [redundant] **outbid one another to get properties. Asking prices did not reflect the high selling prices that properties** garnered ~~most houses were being sold above asking price and above the price that they had been assessed at for sale~~ [wordy and redundant]. It was being called a sellers' market and, suddenly, ~~"fixer-uppers" or~~ [redundant] **"handy man specials"** ~~did not last on the market. They~~ [redundant] **sold as quickly,** ~~if not more quickly, than other~~, as sounder houses. This also had a consequential effect on **what was called entry level housing** ~~or housing for first-time buyers~~ [redundant]. Now, what had been affordable housing **for first-time buyers,** ~~a new young couple starting out~~ [wordy and redundant]~~,~~ was above their means in many **urban markets** ~~in cities~~ [redundant]. Even though the government was telling everyone that inflation was running at a lower rate than it had in years, the housing market ~~was spiralling out of control beyond the reach of many young Canadians~~ **was rising quickly** [wordy and redundant]. Suddenly, banks were offering thirty and thirty-five year mortgages, and people were looking at a future where, if they were to buy into the dream of owning their own house, they would have **no disposable income** ~~no money for holidays or the pleasures in life~~ [wordy and redundant], ~~for a very long time,~~ [wordy or redundant] **until they retired.**

20 errors

Exercise 44-2 Correctness and Diction Levels

In the following answer key, the errors are crossed out. In bold we provide suggestions for eliminating them. You may have handled the errors differently.

One of the unexpected effects of computers in our world is the extent to which they make us ~~airheads~~ **dumb**. A recent experience in a Tim Hortons revealed one way this tendency manifests itself. I was there for the ~~simplistic~~ **simple** task of picking up bagels. When I ordered six bagels, the server hit some keys and ~~asserted~~ **said** the price was $6.60. I have been ~~effecting~~ **making** the same purchase ~~for quite a while~~ **frequently** and therefore corrected her, pointing out that the real price was $3.49. She looked at me with that look that says, "Why do I get stuck with the ~~yahoos~~ **difficult customers**?" and repeated the $6.60 price. I asked her if she would turn around and look at the listed prices and confirm the price for ~~bulky~~ **bulk** bagels. Before very long, she had summoned a co-worker, who punched the same keys and said ~~gimme~~ "**Give me** $6.60." I repeated my suggestion about actually ~~casting their eyeballs on~~ **looking at** [or **examining**] the price list behind them. Eventually, a third worker arrived to clear up the ~~contretemps~~ **argument**. She explained to the other two how a single bagel's price was $1.10, but the special price for a bulk purchase of six to go was $3.49 and required a different sequence of keys. This whole ~~aversion~~ **amusing** experience reminded me how our electronic ~~chum~~ **friend** is also an opponent in its tendency to ~~oppress~~ **suppress** our common sense. We have all had the ~~ha-ha~~ **amusing** experience of being told by a server that we owe some ~~over-the-top~~ **inflated** price for a purchase when we know that figure is wrong. But years of having a machine do the ~~add-and-subtract bit~~ **computing** for us have left us unable to apply our general sense of proportion to numbers. We should know that a burger and a pop can't cost $22.67, but the computer's omniscience befuddles us and we say whatever it tells us to say. This is, you know, not ~~a big deal~~ **too serious** when all we're talking about is a price in a Tim Hortons outlet. But, in 2000, Enron duped tons of Americans (and Canucks too) so badly that we sent its stock price to $90.00 before the truth emerged about what they really had and they became worthless overnight. Their ~~accounting buddies~~ **accountants**, the pros when it comes to numbers, were all part of the Arthur Anderson group and aided in the deception, So that company also ~~went belly up~~ **failed** as a result, as they should have. But where was our common sense? Why didn't we ask them to ~~fess up about~~ **accurately report** their earnings to stock value ratio? More recently, where was our fiduciary common sense when we were investing heavily in selling sub-prime mortgages to people who couldn't qualify for a mortgage ~~in a month of Sundays~~ **because of their income levels**? That "we," of course, included pension funds, ~~brainy~~ **shrewd** bankers, and even our national pension plan ~~sharpies~~ **managers**. At this point you probably think I have ~~extrapolated~~ **elevated** a ~~little bitty~~ **small** point into ~~a big deal~~ an **inflated premise**, but the basic fact remains. We should have been applying our sense of numeric proportion and our basic knowledge about affordability, but we weren't. We get used to relying on some outside agent to make us ~~savvy~~ **knowledgeable** when we should be relying on our own basic sense.

27 errors

Exercise 44-3 Clichés and Idioms

In the following answer key the clichés and idiom problems have been crossed out. More appropriate expressions follow in bold.

Have you seen the television advertisements that ask what seems to be a sincere question: how can seniors turn the fixed equity they have built up in their homes into cash? We have been told that ~~a man's home is his castle~~ **people's homes are important to them**, but, suddenly, in conflict ~~to~~ **with** everything we have been told, financial institutions are telling people who have managed to pay off their debt before retiring that it is now preferable ~~in going~~ **to go** into debt again so that they can spend freely. Rather than having ~~their lifestyle grind to a halt~~ **a more frugal lifestyle** in retirement, they can have ~~an awesome~~ **a fulfilling** life in their ~~golden years~~ **old age** ~~skipping through the tulips and having a ball~~ **enjoying themselves**. Old age and retirement, we are being told, is a time when ~~good things come to those who wait~~ **seniors can do what they want**. It is a time when people can believe firmly that they ~~should not put off to tomorrow what they can do today~~ **should do the things that please them now**.

Financial institutions are actually building ~~upon~~ **on** people's belief that ~~there is no place like home~~ **their home is an essential part of their identity**; they suggest that seniors are ~~painting themselves into a corner~~ **limiting their lifestyle** when they don't need to. After all, the advertisements argue, with the equity they have in their homes, seniors have ~~a bird in the hand, and they don't have to dream about the two in the bush~~ **the means to do what they want**. They are capable ~~to use~~ **of using** the money they have in their houses in accord ~~to~~ **with** their wishes so that they can be independent ~~to~~ **of** those around them. Most often, the programs associated with this line of reasoning are known as CHIPs or Canadian Home Income Plans, but they are also called reverse mortgages. In a reverse mortgage, a senior is told he or she can ~~have a ball~~ enjoy **him or herself** and ~~not have to pay the piper~~ **not have to worry about paying for the loan**. Reverse mortgage advertisements note that seniors do not have to pay any interest on the mortgage as long as they live in their house. They don't, however, tell the senior that, even at prime mortgage rates, the interest on the mortgage will compound quickly. If a senior were to take out a CHIP for $100,000, an amount that looks ~~a safe bet~~ **reasonable** given that a large number of houses cost between $400,000 and $500,000 in Canada, the simple interest on that $100,000 after one year at even 5 percent, would total $5,000. In the second year, the interest would be calculated on $105,000 and be $5,250. Thus, the total amount to be repaid to the lending institution after just ten years would be $162,889.44 with an interest of $7,756.64 in the tenth year. If the senior were to live for twenty years, the interest accrued on the loan would total $165,329.68, and the loan would have a face value of $265,329.68. The question might be who is ~~having their cake and eating it too~~ **benefiting from this plan**, the senior or the bank? It is sad when financial institutions can take advantage of seniors in this manner.

Seniors have to ~~wake up and smell the coffee~~ **understand the financial trap involved** and complain about such deceptions.

20 errors

Chapter 45 Pronoun Case

Exercise 45-1 Pronoun case

In the following answer key, each error is crossed out and the correct form of the pronoun is in bold.

1. The majority of Canadians, ~~me~~ **myself** included, believed that the economic growth of recent years would continue.
2. Our leaders had assured us that they would continue to have balanced budgets for the future and that they would use the surpluses to pay down historical debt. **CORRECT**
3. Those of ~~we~~ **us** who believed them are now aware that the leaders were simply wrong.
4. In early 2009, Stephen Harper, a staunch defender of balanced budgets, tabled a severely unbalanced budget, assuring us citizens that there was no alternative. **CORRECT**
5. Clearly, the rapid decline of market values worldwide had caused ~~him~~ **his** changing his position on deficit spending.
6. When other provincial politicians followed Harper's lead, we knew the conservative belief that governments should not impose ~~their selves~~ **themselves** in the marketplace no longer applied.
7. Apparently, if governments in most industrial countries throw billions of dollars into public and private projects to stimulate a dead economy, it is hard for ~~whomever~~ **whoever** commands a middle power like Canada to resist copying that lead.
8. Gordon Campbell of British Columbia followed the same path and it had been he who insisted that a deficit budget would never be tabled by any government he ran. **CORRECT**
9. In many ways, Canada was simply following the lead of the American president, Barack Obama; it was he who first argued for the transfer of public monies to assist private business and fund economic activity. **CORRECT**
10. No matter what we think of the abandonment of conservative values by conservative politicians, we might applaud the economic stimulus caused by ~~their~~ **them** choosing pragmatism over traditional policy.
    NOTE: A case can be made for both "their" and "them" in this construction; technically, however, the preposition 'by' requires the objective case of "them."

Chapter 46 Pronoun Choice

Exercise 46-1 Pronoun Choice

Part A

The correct answers are in brackets after the alternatives each sentence has given you.

Each spring in Canada, Canadians are bombarded with advertising by financial institutions **which/that/who/whom [that]** advise us all to put money into tax savings plans called RRSPs and RESPs. It is a sure sign that tax season is upon us. **Who/Whom [Who]** can forget the campaign called "Freedom 55" **which/that [, which]** suggested if people put money away every year in an RRSP account, they would be able to retire at the young age of fifty-five rather than the traditional sixty-five? Yet before you put money into one plan or the other, it is important to know **its/their [its]** limitations and strengths. You have to know not only **who/whom [who]** can put money into an RRSP or a RESP but also what advantages each of the plans holds for you.

  The RRSP, the oldest of the two plans, is the one **which/that [that]** most people have heard of. As a February 11, 2008, article by Sarah Dougherty in the *Montreal Gazette* titled "RRSPs Have Come a Long Way Since Introduction in the 1950s" notes, it was Louis St. Laurent's Liberal Party, just before it was defeated by John Diefenbaker's Conservatives, **who/whom/that/which [that]** introduced RRSPs to Canada. At that time, there was no Canada Pension for retirees to depend on, and the government realized that Canadians **who/whom [who]** did not have access to a company pension could easily end up in poverty after they reached the then mandatory retirement age of sixty-five.

  The question many Canadians ask in their youth is when should they start investing in an RRSP. Banks encourage people to place money in RRSP plans as the banks earn money from managing the funds. Interestingly enough, people forget that in many cases, management fees for RRSPs apply even in years when RRSPs lose money. Those **who/whom [who]** put money into RRSPs would be wise to examine the management fees attached to the plan they are interested in to see whether the plan is a good investment for them. Some plans **which/that [that]** advertise their returns do so in ways **which/that [that]** can be deceiving to those **who/whom [who]** are interested in them. As well, those interested in saving money might think about possible alternatives. Placing money in a retirement savings plan **which/that [that]** will give them money upon retirement may not be a priority if they have other, more pressing financial needs. People have to think about **who/whom [whom]** they are giving the money to and whether they have a pressing need **which/that [that]** should be met now. After all, students paying taxes at the rate of 18 percent should realize that all they are going to defer is the tax on the money they place in an RRSP. There is a likelihood that their marginal tax rate, if they end up getting a good job after they have finished their education, will eventually put them in a tax bracket that is higher than 18 percent when they retire. There is more than one way of looking at RRSP plans; that is something **whoever/whomever [whoever]** considers them should know.

Part B

The errors are crossed out. The correct answers are in bold.

In good times, RRSPs may be the vehicle of choice for those ~~that~~ **who** wish to save for their retirement, but with a host of products out there, many of which look like one another, the question most people have is "Which should I choose?" Questions like this are not simple to answer. An examination of the many plans ~~which~~ **that** are in the marketplace could be time consuming. As well, an RRSP product that has performed well in the past may not perform well in the future. Investors ~~whom~~ **who** have examined the different plans know that comparing one RRSP option with another is like comparing apples and oranges. Anyone ~~that~~ **who** is investing in an RRSP should consider both the mix of assets in a plan and the plan's Management Expense Ratio or MER. It is not worthwhile to invest in a secure RRSP plan ~~which~~ **that** will bring you an extremely low return when that return all but disappears once the MER is applied. In a case like this, whatever you do in an RRSP might be worse for you than what you could do outside of an RRSP. Whoever said choosing a good RRSP was simple?

5 errors

Chapter 48 Inclusive Language

Exercise 48-1 Inclusive Language

You may come up with a number of different corrections to the passage as it challenges you to deal with some sensitive issues. In the answer key the expressions that need to be revised are underlined. Appropriate answers have been included in brackets after them. You may find other solutions for the problems in this passage and may want to discuss your solutions with your instructor.

You are saving a down payment for the purchase of your own condo, your own castle. You remember that **every man** ["everyone" or "every person"] looks forward to being **the master of his domain** [in charge of his or her domain], a **king** [monarch] in **his** [his or her] own realm. Everyone looks to a future when **he** [he or she – but, preferably, you could change "Everyone" to "People" and "he" to "they" to avoid the "he or she" awkwardness] can gaze out on **his** [his or her – alternative: their] backyard complete with BBQ, deck, and gardens and enjoy the privacy that the fruits of **his** [his or her – alternative: their] labour have given **him** [him or her – alternative: them]. Yes indeed, there is no place like home. Young couples look forward to having a place of their own, complete with a two-car garage, a big-screen television, pets, and a child or two. Even though our cousins to the south might think we live in **igloos like Eskimos** [igloos, the traditional Inuit housing], in general, housing in Canada is very similar to housing in the U.S. Yes, **mankind has** [people or humans have] come a long way from the days when a handy cave made a good home.

Yet the modern Canadian family unit is living in a more complex community than it did in the past and thinks of housing differently than previous generations. Urbanites in Canada, in fact, live in a complex, blended culture. Instead of looking forward to owning a suburban rancher, having two children, and being surrounded by people from the same ethnic background, modern urban Canadians who are purchasing their own residence are more likely to live in a condo close to the urban core and be surrounded by a variety of peoples and a variety of neighbours, including **homosexual** [lesbian and gay male] couples and families from a wide range of ethnic backgrounds, such as those from the **Indo-Canadian**, **Oriental**, and **Afro-Canadian** [South Asian, Asian, and Black] communities. In fact, when a community organization forms, it is not unlikely that the **chairman** [chair or chairperson] of the organization has to recognize the complex elements in the organization and the complex nature of his [his or her] urban neighbourhood. When organizing community events, the chairman [chair or chairperson] has to be wary of **old wives' tales** [superstition] and be careful **to man** [staff] and run programs with care to ensure that the programs are not exclusionary to people who have **different sexual preferences** [a different sexual orientation].

18 errors

Chapter 50 Active and Passive Voice

Exercise 50-1 Active and Passive Voice

Please note that the following are only suggested versions. You may have written your corrections differently. The critical element here is that you converted sentences written in passive voice into sentences written in active voice.

1. Recently, newspapers reported a remarkable scam that affected a large number of people.
2. Most notably, once this scheme surfaced publicly, we learned that the investors had lost 65 billion dollars.

3. Investigators identified the fraud as a "Ponzi scheme," a fraud that uses the money from one investor to make a payment to an earlier investor.
4. This particular kind of swindle is also known as a pyramid scheme, a deception that makes time payments to early investors from the money spent by later investors, ensuring that the investors know nothing until investments cease.
5. The news accounts of the fraud highlighted the two facts that many investors were high-profile people and that the total loss recorded was the largest ever attributed to a pyramid scheme.
6. High-profile New Yorkers, a major New York charity, well-known Hollywood people, and even the retired manager of a hedge fund were only a few of the thousands of defrauded investors.
7. The elaborate deception was the reported cause of at least one suicide, an investor who had put over a billion dollars into this fake investment.
8. The perpetrator of this pyramid scheme, Bernard Madoff, was a New Yorker who had been a well-respected figure in the New York social world.
9. The maintenance of such a simple fraud for so long and the duping of so many supposedly sophisticated investors remain central mysteries in this whole affair.
10. Ironically, the scheme would still be going on if it hadn't been exposed accidentally when many investors attempted to recover their monies to cover losses incurred by the general implosion of the American economy at the end of 2008.

Part X PUNCTUATION

Chapter 52 The Comma

Exercise 52-1 The Comma

Part A

An article in *Maclean's* titled "This Computer Is So Me"[1] sums up the problems of the age only too well: mass manufacturers have realized that people prize their individuality. They don't want to dress the same as everyone else[,] buy the same food[,] or think the same thoughts. As such[,] corporations are trying to stress that their products[,] whether they be hamburgers, computers[,] or automobiles[,] can be customized to suit every individual's taste. It seems[ ] we've come a long way from Henry Ford's comment about the Model T Ford: "You can have it any color you like, as long as it's black." Ford was interested in producing automobiles that everyone could afford. He believed people would accept mass-produced products. Currently[,] people seem to be rebelling against the fact that manufacturers can produce goods cheaply[,] as long as they have large production runs and an efficient production line. The irony lies in the fact that people still want to pay mass-production prices for goods that appear to be custom made. That is the secret to contemporary marketing and advertising. Today[,] as the *Maclean's* article notes, corporations want you to think you are making decisions that personalize what you are buying. All the way from the lowly hamburger to the expensive automobile, corporations are giving you choices that make it seem like you are in control[,] you are making the decisions. The slogans that they are using to reinforce this are emblematic of that sensibility. "Choose to have it your way[,]" Burger King's slogan[,] is even prominently displayed on the corporation website at the top of the nutrition page. However[,] the use of you or[,] in this case[,] me is not new to the advertising world. Macdonald's use of slogans that put you[,] the individual consumer[,] in the centre of their advertisements started in 1967 when they used the slogan "McDonald's is Your Kind of Place" and followed that up with the 1971 slogan[,] the one people remember even today[,] "You Deserve a Break Today."

20 errors

Part B

The issue of targeting people's desire to be individual is not limited to inexpensive items like fast food. It goes far beyond that. As Lianne George points out in her article adapted from the book she wrote with Steve Maich[,] *The Ego Boom: Why the World Really Does Revolve Around You*[,] corporations like Dell Computers have taken the concept and applied it to the purchase of computers online. Dell[,] which is famous for its online computer sales[,] saw the retail market becoming flat[,] but the company quickly noticed that what people wanted was choice; they did not all want the same things in their computer. Rather than giving people a standard computer that would include items most users wanted[,] Dell decided to build sales and computers using an online decision tree. At the bottom of the tree[,] customers are faced with basic choices including the size of the hard drive[,] the size of the RAM[,] the types of drives[,] and the type of chip used to run the computer. After that[,] the choices include what type of software the buyer wants, the type of monitor[,] the size of the monitor[,] and the screen's definition. As prospective customers add items they want to their "custom built computer[,]" they can see how each item affects the total price. Buying a computer with Dell's online site, as opposed to going into a store and searching out the one that is right for you[,]suddenly[] becomes a totally different experience. Not only can prospective customers tailor their computer to their needs[,] but, once they have finished "assembling" their personal computer[,] they will then receive step-by-step e-mails telling them that their computer is being ordered[,] assembled[,] packed[,] and[,] finally[,] shipped to them. Although Dell has copied the concept of personalizing that has been utilized by others, it has done so in a unique way that makes the decision tree on its website one that reinforces the idea that consumers are "customizing" their purchase to their needs. Henry Ford couldn't have done it better. Dell figured out how to let consumers[,] utilizing the decision tree[,] get the assembly line to produce exactly what they want. Nothing is wasted; Dell does not even need retail outlets to produce sales.

25 errors

Chapters 53 and 54 The Semicolon and the Colon

Exercise 53/54-1 The Semicolon and the Colon

In the following answer key the correct placement of the semicolon or colon is indicated by the use of the word that precedes that placement. Also, the added punctuation is bracketed in the actual sentence.

1. It is impossible to read the daily news and not be struck by the irony implicit in many reports[;] frequently, we see that our attempts to control events fail.

   reports;

2. The reason for the irony is always the same[:] our planning doesn't take in enough factors.

   same:

3. A recent example from the *Vancouver Sun* illustrates this phenomenon[;] in this instance, good planning failed to anticipate what the future might bring.

   phenomenon;

4. Vancouver enjoys a significant business in unloading shipping containers for several reasons[:] it is the largest western port in Canada, it is relatively close to large Asian economies, and it has access to the major cross-Canada highway.

   reasons:

5. Consequently, Vancouver and Prince Rupert have both expanded their port facilities[;] behind this assumption was the expectation that West Coast ports would continue to enjoy expanding container business.

   facilities;

6. However, this assumption did not factor in three developments[:] the Panama Canal is being significantly widened, global warming is increasing the likelihood that our Northwest Passage will be open water in the summertime, and transportation by water is the cheapest means of moving containers of goods.

   developments:

7. There is also another factor at play here**[:]** the largest density of people in North America live in the east of Canada and the United States.

   here:

8. This means the largest markets and industrial zones are also in the east**[;]** typically, therefore, this is the main destination for containers and the products they hold.

   east;

9. Given the fact that transportation by water is much less expensive than transportation by road, Asian business may soon have several options**[:]** they can, if they wish, ship containers directly to eastern North American markets using the widened Panama Canal**[;]** they may even be able to use the Northwest Passage, open most of last summer, to reach our eastern cities**[;]** or they can renegotiate the fees currently in effect by threatening not to use our port any more.

   options: Canal; cities;

10. Naturally, we did not anticipate these developments when we committed to expansion of our container capacity**[;]** equally, we couldn't predict that a worldwide recession would diminish the number of containers being shipped from countries like China to Canada's west coast.

    capacity;

11. This is, therefore, the basis of the irony**[:]** with the best of intentions and careful planning, we commit to a plan of action that turns out to be questionable.

    irony:

12. As the *Sun* column pointed out, American ports like Long Beach/Los Angeles have already experienced a decline in traffic**[;]** it is distinctly possible that our expanded port facilities will end up serving fewer customers rather than more.

    traffic;

Chapter 55 Quotation Marks

Exercise 55-1 Quotation Marks

In the following answer key the corrected punctuation, where necessary, is noted below each sentence.

1. "Can you believe how picky the officials were at the halfpipe competition?", asked most of the competitors at the snowboard test event hosted by Cypress Mountain, near the city of Vancouver.

   It should be **halfpipe competition?" asked** most of the competitors; delete the comma here.

Answer Key   221

2. Cypress Mountain officials defended their cancellation of the parallel giant slalom by stating: "We feared there was not enough time to get the area designated for the event ready in accordance with international specifications. Additionally, we have to serve our own members, and it was our view that they would not have appreciated losing another afternoon on what they regard as their hill. You have to remember that this is just a test event to see how the area can be set up for an Olympic event."

    The quotation here is longer than fours sentences (MLA), so it must be indented ten spaces and segregated from the speaker tag, with a line separating the quotation both above and below. The parenthetic reference would follow the period or other punctuation mark that concludes the quotation.

3. I did hear one person attending the event observe, "Why does a great event like this have to be brought down by officialdom?"

    CORRECT

4. One of the headlines on the blog of a person who attended reinforced this view read, "great scenery, picky people in charge."

    This is a headline and should be capitalized as in **"Great Scenery, Picky People in Charge"**.

5. On the CTV show *Sunday Sports Highlights*, the cameras emphasized the spectacular surroundings pleasing all who attended this event.

    The title of the television show should be in roman type and placed in quotation marks, as in 'the CTV show, **"Sunday Sports Highlights,"** the cameras'.

6. It is equally interesting to hear the number of critical comments made by traditionalists who lament the decision to include halfpipe and snowboardcross events in the Winter Olympics, feeling this decision represents a foolish Xification of the Olympic competition.

    The invented word **"Xification"** must be placed in quotation marks to show its special character.

7. One element that received no criticism was the judges' decision in the halfpipe competition that gave Shaun White first place. In the words of one impressed fellow competitor, Shaun's run was seriously sick.

    Here, **"sick"** is a slang term and should be placed in quotation marks.

8. Many observers also stressed, after looking more closely at the hundreds of fans watching the competition: "where are all the forty and fifty year olds"?

   The first word of the quotation should be capitalized, as in, "competition: **'Where are'**.

9. Certainly, the crowds were predominantly people in their teens and twenties, dressed in clothes reminiscent of the dress of the competitors, talking in a special language about the halfpipe being under vert, an expression apparently referring to the vertical lips of the halfpipe run.

   The special term **"under vert,"** has to be placed in quotation marks.

10. Overall, the event was a qualified success; in the words of one snowboarder, it was a happening, and it showed the world we have arrived, so get used to us.

    This should be punctuated **"It was . . . get used to us."**

Chapter 56 The Apostrophe

Exercise 56-1 The Apostrophe

The corrections in the passage are in bold and underlined.

It started off simply enough. It **wasn't** even something that people paid much attention to. After all, the apostrophe is such an insignificant punctuation mark. Who **would've** thought that it would come to the point where a city in Britain, Birmingham, decided to officially drop the apostrophe from all its road signs. A friend of ours, Maureen, sent us an article in the *Globe and Mail,* "Trust the British to Make Apostrophes a Class Issue," that comments on **Birmingham's** decision and notes one of the reasons why Birmingham **thinks** the apostrophe should be dropped from street names is GPS units that **can't** locate streets on a map if there is an apostrophe in the name. In **Birmingham's** case, "St. Paul's Square," for instance, is being changed to "St. Pauls Square" so that the GPS units can recognize the location. One of the Birmingham **counsellors** observes that, as the street names in question are no longer owned by anyone, there is no need to use the apostrophe, but, more to the point, he argued that apostrophes "confuse people. If I want to go to a restaurant, I don't want to have an A-level in English to find it."

When Nav Sangha, a former student of mine, sent me a copy of Lynne **Truss's** book *Eats Shoots and Leaves*, I was fascinated. Truss points to the fact that, in Britain, the apostrophe has been abused for a long time, and it **isn't** just the possessive apostrophe that is not being used properly. She gives examples like "Ladie's hairdresser," and "Freds' restaurant" to illustrate the kinds of mistakes people are making with possession (52). She notes that people are confused about when to use "whose" and "who's" as well (61). **Who's** right, you might ask? We ought to know; it **isn't** that difficult.

Common in both Britain and Canada are misuse problems in business advertising and signs. Next time you pass a **McDonald's**, look at the **restaurant's** sign. Then look at a Tim **Hortons** sign. When you do, you will know who uses the possessive form correctly. You will also know how, using the two **corporations**' spellings, to correct these two names to assign possession correctly for this exercise. Then you can go online to Google and check for the correct spelling of the **Hudson's** Bay Company and the store Timothy Eaton started, Eaton's. More recent corporations tend to be at fault more often. For instance, the western Canadian restaurant Earls leaves out the apostrophe. It is no wonder that people are confused. **It's** all around us, signs that don't follow the rules for possession and the use of the apostrophe!

17 errors

Chapters 57, 58, 60 The Slash; Parentheses; The Dash

Exercise 57/58/60-1 The Slash, the Dash, and Parentheses

In the following answer key the correct punctuation is given following each sentence, with the words preceding and following that punctuation included.

1. Watching the X-games on television reminds me that these games conceived in the last five years and passionately adopted by a special subculture are specifically designed to appeal to a young audience.

    … games—**conceived** in the last five years … **subculture**—are

2. The *Winter Games* version is offered in both night and day versions the latter possible only through strong lighting and physically limited venues that allow the television channels to appeal to both a daytime and a nighttime audience.

    … **versions (**the latter [. . .] limited venues**) that** …

3. One of the signs that the audience for this invented sport is young is the unique designs of the boardsharnesses used for the different competitions.

    … the **boards/harnesses** used …

4. They are designed for short, stubby "skis" that have the capacity to turn sharply, to glide easily, to hold the boots to the "skis" during jumps and flips, and perhaps the key element to work within more tightly-defined spaces than regular skis can do.

   … and **(perhaps the key element)** to …

5. During the 2008 2009 season of the Winter X games, I watched several competitions and noted the distinctive dimensions of this new winter sport.

   … the **2008/2009** season …

6. The competitors average age twenty-three virtually all had nicknames that reflected their status in what amounted to a counterculture and hair styles that echoed that culture and their youth.

   … competitors **(average age twenty-three)** virtually …

7. The two forms of competition I watched, snowboardcross and halfpipe, both echoed and as I saw it contrasted with the regular competitions they echoed.

   … and **(as I saw it)** contrasted … [NOTE: it could also be … and—**as I saw it**—contrasted …]

8. The halfpipe consisted of a U-shaped run cut in the snow that allowed the competitors to perform complex air manoeuvres in the tradition of gymnastics, while probably the intention limiting the run to a completion of the downhill length of that U-shaped run.

   … while **(probably the intention)** limiting …

9. The competitors in this run must move strictly from side to side of the run, launching themselves into the air through the aid of the sharply vertical sides to the wonder and applause of the watching crowd and constantly advancing down the length of the run.

   … sides—**to the** wonder and applause of the watching crowd—**and** …

10. The snowboardcross competition featured the contestants in helmets and different-coloured bibs racing over small hills and around curves over what appeared to be a half-mile course to see who could come first or second or third actually in the heats and advance to the final.

    … first **(or** second or third actually in the **heats) and** …

Chapter 52-60 Punctuation

Exercise 52/60-2 Punctuation Review

In the following answer key the corrections have been placed in brackets. In some cases there is more than one way of correcting the punctuation errors. Consult your instructor if you have done something different to correct an error.

There is one famous quotation that everyone who has watched the old movie *Field of Dreams* remembers. This catchy little quotation becomes emblematic of the core theme of the movie [— or ,] a theme that actually reflects human behaviour over the past twenty years as we build bigger[,] more complex communities. It seems innocuous at first[,] and slightly silly[,] when Kevin Costner[']s character Ray Kinsella[ ] hears a voice that intones a vague comment[:] "If you build it, he will come." He does not completely understand this comment[,] a comment he eventually links to building a baseball field on his farm. Yet this comment sets the tone for the strongest set of fantasies about land development and ownership of the past twenty years. I hadn[']t realized how this film related to the trends of the past twenty years until just recently[,] but we all know that development drives population movement. Remember the last scene of the film[?] After the baseball field has been built[ ] and the main character has played catch with his long dead father[,] the camera pans back and shows a long line of car lights heading up the road to the Kinsella farm in the middle of Iowa. From this image[,] we are supposed to infer that the farm[']s future has been secured[:] the dream has been realized[,] and the family will live happily ever after. Something eerily similar has happened to our society[. O]ver the past twenty years[,] people have bought into the dream that, if they buy property[,] the prices will keep going up[;] if they want better roads for their commute into the urban centre or out to the suburbs[,] bigger[,] wider roads and bridges will be built to accommodate the increased volume of traffic. No one has stopped to think about what all this does to the land the city occupies[,] to land utilization[,] or to urban sprawl[,] which generates many energy inefficiencies. Instead[,] everyone simply wants one thing[: or ,] to "live happily ever after."

   Maybe it is time we started to look at urban development and our expectations through a different lens[;] maybe we need to rethink our lifestyles[,] our way of living, and use a different set of values when planning our communities and[ ] our residences. You only have to ask yourself one question to prove that this is so[:] what happens if we do nothing and continue building our urban communities and their surrounding suburbs the way we have over the past two decades[?]

   To understand what is happening, all one has to do is look at the density of Canada[']s urban centres and compare the density of these cities to other urban centres in the world. According to the website citymayors.com[,] Canada's largest city[,] Toronto had[,] in January[,] 2007[,] a population density of 2,650 people per square kilometre and a total population of 4,367,000. At this time[,] it was the 97th most densely populated city in the world. The most densely populated city[,] which had 29,650 people per square kilometre and a total population of 14,350,000 people[,] was Mumbai, India. Madrid[,] Spain[,] which had a slightly bigger population than Toronto with 4,900,000 people[,] had a population density of 5,200 people per square kilometre and was the 42nd most densely populated city in the world. Vancouver, Canada[']s third largest city[,] for all its boasts about being strongly connected to the environment and environmentalism[,] had a population density of 1,650 people per square kilometre[,] with a total population of 1,830,000 people[,] and was 123rd in the list for urban density.

How we deal with urban density will not only decide whether our cities are sustainable but also whether they will suffer from urban blight and degradation of the surrounding hinterland. The development of cities has too often been subject to the whims of developers[,] who have short[-]term gains in mind[,] not long[-]term goals. They are not interested in the future of the cities they help develop[;] they are interested in the future of their bottom line. Sadly[,] quite a number of cities have councils dominated by individuals who have ties to realtors and developers[,] and this has meant that town planning has not always been governed by sustainable principles[. I]nstead[,] planning has been governed by greed. Because of this problem[,] the future of our largest urban centres and their densities is not being governed by principles that augur well for the future. Would an investigation of whether cities follow the principles of good governance be in order[?] Would it be a good idea for cities to consider the relationship between development, density, and future problems[?] Should cities be judged on how they deal with urban blight[,] urban poverty[?] The bottom line is, cities have to think about the future now. What roads[,] transportation systems[,] housing density[,] and industry cities put in place today will define the infrastructure and urban problems of the future.

Comma added: 42
No punctuation needed: 3
Semicolon errors: 3
Colon errors: 4
Question mark errors: 5
Hyphen errors: 2
Apostrophe errors: 5
Period: 2
Dash errors: 1 (could be a comma though)

Part XI MECHANICS

Chapter 63 Capitalization

Exercise 63-1 Capitalization

1. When the Olympics are opened to the world in February 2010, we can expect Stephen Harper, our **Prime Minister**, and Premier Gordon Campbell of B.C. to be prominent in the official ceremonies.

    "Prime Minister" should not be capitalized.

2. The opening ceremonies are scheduled for BC **place**, the stadium built more than twenty years ago and scheduled to be refurbished following the Olympic **games** of 2010.

    Here, "place" is a part of the proper noun and must be capitalized; "games" must also be capitalized.

3. One of the most interesting venues for these games will be the Richmond **olympic speed-skating oval**, the building designed to house the long-track speed-skating competitions.

    This should properly read "Richmond Olympic Speed-Skating Oval".

4. This building was opened in 2009 by Mayor Malcolm Brodie, one of the more prominent **Mayors** in metropolitan Vancouver.

    "Mayors" should not be capitalized.

5. "While the short-term function of this building will be to house Olympic events," announced Brodie at the opening, "**We** know that it will eventually be a major community centre for many activities."

    "We" is part of the quotation and should not be capitalized.

6. The Oval is a spectacular building visually and a provocative building politically.

    CORRECT

7. It first gained political fame because the originally estimated cost of $50 to 60 million became $180 million upon completion; the Richmond **city council** took heat for the escalation of costs.

    Here, "city council" is part of a proper noun and should be capitalized.

8. Additionally, it was built on a flood plain; this caused problems for a building required to meet rigorous **Specifications** dictated by the Olympic **speed-skating council**.

   "Specifications" should not be capitalized; "speed-skating council" should be.

9. One of its unique features is the arched roof whose interior is finished with wood reclaimed from trees killed by the **Pine Beetle** infestation that attacked B.C. forests some years ago.

   "Pine Beetle" should not be capitalized

10. This enormous roof has attracted international attention and was a source of great pride for Vanoc, the Vancouver Olympic **committee** charged with responsibility for all the **olympic** facilities.

    The word "committee" is part of the proper term and should be capitalized; "olympic" should also be capitalized.

11. Unfortunately, while a brilliant visual effect, the roof was found to have major water penetration problems, and the dispute is ongoing about whether the repairs should be paid for by Richmond **city council**, Vanoc, **the roofing construction association** of B.C., or the builder.

    Capitalize "city council" and "roofing construction association".

    Not surprisingly, other **Municipalities** in B.C.'s Lower Mainland are secretly happy they are not involved; they are interested in seeing how it will all turn out.

    "Municipalities" should not be capitalized. (Note: Lower Mainland is often capitalized.)

12. In the meantime, B.C.'s **liberals** and **new democrats** are keeping as far away from the dispute as they can, and the provincial legislature has had no comment.

    The names of political parties, such as "Liberals" and "New Democrats," are capitalized.

13. The Richmond public has spoken, however; they turned out in large numbers to the opening, skated on the **Oval** track as soon as they could, and made it clear to the Richmond **city council** that all Richmond citizens should be proud of this striking Olympic and **City** facility.

    Here, "Oval" is an adjective and should not be capitalized; "city council" should be capitalized; "City" should not be capitalized.

14. Perhaps most important, the **international** Olympic Committee gave their unanimous approval of the oval when they toured it in the spring of 2009.

    In this case, "international" is part of the proper noun and must be capitalized

Chapter 64 Abbreviations

Exercise 64-1 Abbreviations

The correct abbreviations are in bold in each sentence.

1. **Alta.** is the abbreviation for the province that has, as its two main cities, Edmonton and Calgary.
2. **Professor Higgins** is the name of the central male character in *My Fair Lady*.
3. **Gov. Gen.** Michaëlle Jean was born in Haiti, and French is her first language.
4. When you write a letter in Canada and you are sending it to Newfoundland, you must make sure you use the proper Canada Post abbreviation, which is **NL**.
5. There is a strong history of documentary film production in Canada, and, historically, most of those films were made by the National Film Board of Canada, which is most often referred to as the **NFB**.
6. If there is a strike in Ottawa, the government most often speaks with the leaders of the Canadian Union of Public Employees or **CUPE**, a union representing about a half million workers.
7. Though in the past, the most common practice in Canada was to designate dates using the Christian era signifiers **AD** and **BC**, today the more acceptable era designations are **BCE** and **CE**, which stand for Before the Common Era and Common Era respectively.
8. When introduced as [**Dr. Marvin Gold** or **Marvin Gold Ph.D**.], Dr. Gold always felt as if his credentials were overwhelming his personal identity.
9. Now that most popular style manuals no longer use Latinate terms, it is vary rare that you see such terms as **loc. cit.**, which is the abbreviation for the Latin *loco citato* and means "in the place cited."
10. Federal political parties in Canada may carry the same names or similar names as provincial parties. If ever you were unsure of whether they stood for the same policies federally and provincially, you had only to look at the political views of the federal **NDP** and some of the provincial parties by the same name. How much in common the **BQ** in Ottawa has with the **PQ** in Quebec might be another interesting question. Similarly, the Liberal party and the Conservatives certainly have different agendas provincially and federally.

Chapter 65 Numbers

Exercise 65-1 Numbers

In the following answer key, the corrections are given sentence by sentence.

1. Correct.
2. "1 trillion dollars"
3. "$2 trillion"
4. "$3 trillion"
5. Correct.
6. Correct.
7. Correct.
8. "100,000 years"
9. Correct.
10. Should be "$80,000"
11. "$1 trillion", "AD 12502010", "January 1".
12. Correct.
13. "4 percent", "$3,333,333,333.33."
14. Correct.
15. "$3,000,000,000."
16. Should be "$3,333.33."
17. "billions of dollars"
18. Correct.

Chapter 66 Hyphens

Exercise 66-1 Hyphens

Part A

I have decided we are living in a very strange, **out-of-touch** world. Students in British Columbia are paying more in tuition fees per year than corporations in the province are paying in taxes. It seems we have, as a society, decided that it is more important to support the bottom line of businesses than to support the future of our country or **first-class** education for the next generation of Canadians. In effect, we are supporting an implicit class system whereby the wealthy can afford to have their offspring educated in the best **state-of-the-art** jobs. In contrast, the poor and the middle class will have to go into

Answer Key   231

debt or have their children go into debt to manage to get a decent education and a **quasi-decent** job. How sad is this? On top of this, we have people now supporting negative population growth wherein a whole generation will not produce offspring. Someone needs to rethink the consequences of these ideals for the next generation. We are creating a society that is **anti-family**, **anti-education**, and **anti-democratic**. Is it **old-fashioned** to think about the family unit and its future? We are creating a society where the few will have much, the many will have **next to nothing**, and the people who have reached the not so golden years after retirement will not be supported by government programs as the country will be missing a whole generation of young people and, therefore, a whole generation of people who are working and paying taxes. Have we suddenly forgotten what a social contract is? Do we no longer believe in family or **extended-family** groupings? How fragmented and **dysfunctional** are we prepared to let our society become in the name of support for corporate bottom lines and fuzzy notions about sustainability?

11 errors

Part B

A quick look at the cost of a **post-secondary** education[1] is very informative. We think it is important for young adults to have skills that are **up to date**. Even knowing how to use a word processing program and how to use e-mail[1] to send and receive documents are essential skills that students must have at the beginning of their studies. If they don't have computer and **online** skills, they may find themselves disadvantaged when it comes to course selection or course availability. Out of **thirty-five** courses a student may want to take, he or she may find that as many as ten may only be offered **online**. This fact may put a course out of reach for a student who does not have the requisite computer skills. It may sound **self-evident**, but access at home to a computer, just like access to a supportive family, may make or break a student's performance. We may think it **un-Canadian** that people be discriminated against because of their **socio-economic** background, but it is a fact of life today in Canada, in the same way that where people live may affect their ability to get a good education and a good job.

8 errors

Note: The number of words that are hyphenated is changing rapidly. In the 2007 edition of the *Shorter Oxford English Dictionary*, 16,000 words lost their hyphen. Some previously hyphenated words became two words; some became compound words. Post-secondary/postsecondary and e-mail/email are words that currently are spelt two ways. Be careful when using the hyphen. Check a current dictionary when you are in doubt. http://www.reuters.com/article/oddlyEnoughNews/idUSHAR15384620070921?sp=true